# DMITRI
# SHOSTAKOVICH

# CLASSIC *f*M LIFELINES

# DMITRI SHOSTAKOVICH

## AN ESSENTIAL GUIDE TO HIS LIFE AND WORKS

### STEPHEN JACKSON

PAVILION

First published in Great Britain in 1997 by
PAVILION BOOKS LIMITED
26 Upper Ground, London SE1 9PD


Copyright © Pavilion Books Ltd 1997
Front cover illustration © The Lebrecht Collection

Edited and designed by Castle House Press, Penarth, South Wales
Cover designed by Bet Ayer

A CIP catalogue record for this book is available
from the British Library

ISBN 1 86205 016 3

Set in Lydian and Caslon
Printed and bound in Great Britain by Mackays of Chatham

2 4 6 8 10 9 7 5 3 1

This book can be ordered direct from the publisher.
Please contact the Marketing Department.
But try your bookshop first.

# ACKNOWLEDGMENTS

With thanks to Richard at BMG, Katherine and Kerry at EMI, Paul at Chandos, Karen at Koch International, Carole at Sony and the staff at Harmonia Mundi – for the splendid and rarefied feats of altruism that make a project of this sort possible.

# Contents

## A NOTE FROM THE EDITORS

A biography of this type inevitably contains numerous references to pieces of music. The paragraphs are also peppered with 'quotation marks', since much of the tale is told through reported speech.

Because of this, and to make things more accessible for the reader as well as easier on the eye, we decided to simplify the method of typesetting the names of musical works. Conventionally this is determined by the nature of the individual work, following a set of rules whereby some pieces appear in italics, some in italics and quotation marks, others in plain roman type and others still in roman and quotation marks.

In this book, the names of all musical works are simply set in italics. Songs and arias appear in italics and quotation marks.

# SHOSTAKOVICH AND THE SOVIETS

P op Art, that fifteen-minute wonder, first alerted us to the media's ravening maw. Each gesture with our remote control brings us another swarm of ephemera from the television tube, an electronic landscape of filtered data, in which knowledge has been nagged to death and ground down to pap. We find ourselves cloyed by a surfeit of easy cultural icons: a montage gone stale, in which every frame and context has been identified, listed and impaled upon wire.

Games entice us, in this world that is known because it is predictable. We find ourselves disarmed – and it suits us. Suddenly there is the allure of discovery beyond the commonplace, of a higher and secret language. Gone are the days when truth was self-evident in the black ink between staves, when a composer's motivation was simply beside the point. The media age brings us celebrity, our complicity with the star of the show's innermost thoughts, the intimacy and exclusivity of the confessional. So what can it have been like to survive in the travesty of a culture that inspired Orwell's *Nineteen Eighty-Four*: a clapped-out theme park where none of the rides worked and one could be excommunicated for not wanting a go on the dodgems: where secret police reigned supreme, where a citizen's benevolent grin of endorsement for the latest Five-Year Plan could not be allowed for an instant to slip: where one man could sign twelve thousand death-warrants in a single day, where the greatest symphonist of the mid-twentieth century had to sleep with bags packed beside his bed, in case the military wanted to drag him away to an unmarked grave sanctioned by the people, prepared for him in their name – simply because he wrote 'formalist' music?

Of Soviet Russia's death-toll, as Nikita Krushchev later admitted, 'no-one was keeping count'. We have a victim's account of Josef Stalin on the prowl, capricious and cruel and expedient, about to act: 'the pale yellow stare of a predator. He foamed at the mouth and raged.' We have records of Stalin's most ignominious stunt, which he inflicted with relish on his cultural commissar, Tikhon Khrennikov, as indeed on so many:

> As head of the Composers' Union, Khrennikov had to submit the composer candidates to Stalin for the annual Stalin Prize. Stalin had the final say and it was he who chose the names from the list. This took place in his office. Stalin was working – or pretending to work. In any case, he was writing. Khrennikov mumbled names from the list in an optimistic tone. Stalin didn't look up and went on writing. Khrennikov finished reading. Silence.
>
> Suddenly Stalin raised his head and peered at Khrennikov. As people say, 'He put his eye on him'. They say that Stalin had worked out this tactic very well. Anyway, the hereditary shop assistant felt a warmth deep from the bowels of the earth, which scared him even more. He jumped up and backed towards the door, muttering something. 'Our administrator' backed all the way to the reception area where he was grabbed by two hearty male nurses, who were specially trained and knew what to do. They dragged Khrennikov off to a special room, where they undressed him, cleaned him up and put him down on a cot to get his breath. They scrubbed his trousers in the meanwhile. After all, he was a bureaucrat. It was a routine operation. Stalin's opinion on the candidates for the Stalin Prize was conveyed to him later. As we see, heroes do not emerge very well. . . . To crap your pants in front of the leader and teacher is not something that everyone achieves: it's a kind of honour, a higher delight and a higher degree of adulation.
>
> Stalin liked hearing these things about himself. He liked to know that he inspired such fear in his intelligentsia, his artists. After all, they were directors, writers, composers, the builders of

*a new world, a new man. What did Stalin call them? Engineers
of human souls.*

What was it that the poetess, Anna Akhmatova, called Leningrad's railway sidings during the great purges of the 1930s? 'The
asylums of the mad.'

The plight of Dmitri Shostakovich (dragged as he was through
newsreels, vilified in the pages of *Pravda*) shows us a society where
propaganda was the highest aspiration of art, a technology of
exploitation the goal of science: where every utterance was false,
every move part of a puppet-show of brinkmanship and betrayal.
No Soviet composer was the stylistic voyeur that Igor Stravinsky
could afford to be – now that he was in the west out of harm's
way. For California's prime adopted son, alienation was chic:
machine-music an amusing conceit to negate the paraphernalia
of emotion. But for Shostakovich, the rattle of treadmills is a way
of hinting at what is otherwise unthinkable.

Now, propaganda is the half-silvered looking-glass through
which each of us convinces himself that he touches reality. It is
not the dead generations, which to Marx weighed like a nightmare on the imagination of the living; but the mental furniture,
the symbols of solidarity and worth, by which peoples across the
industrialized world reassure themselves that they own truth
itself. It is an iconography of delusion. And it has never been a
characteristic of dreams to admit self-scrutiny, let alone realism,
let alone wit. Dreams are a phosphorescent wash of platitudes,
or else instant and still-born fossils; and they lay bare an under-
current of jingoistic self-regard like nothing else. Yet freedom
means the freedom to make mistakes, and for an artist who needs
to cultivate an outlook of his own, propaganda offers only private
extinction. It is not art, and it comes close only when it acknowledges at least the possibility of despair. That option, more than
anything, is the reason for the greatness of this century's Soviet
music, in spite of all odds; and for the collapse of the ideology
that gave it birth.

When I call Shostakovich a grotesque composer, I mean it as
the highest praise. The grating incongruity of one view of our
world, pitted against another, has always thrown up the most
troublesome and fertile artistic enigmas – from *Antony and Cleo-
patra* and *Cosi fan tutte*, to Kafka with his half-light of ambivalence,

where dissonance forces new scrutiny, new understanding. It establishes the conditions for a filter that can make sense of experience: it engenders a portrait of crisis with the power to create meaning afresh. An ability to generate new language is art's central, crucial feature – and with it, a capacity to forge an architecture that sweeps aside our old imagination. To do this, artists calculate and confront themselves. They see their work as an outsider does. When such a thing happens, a trade in options and meanings is on the cards, where the flawless logic of the absurd contributes to the act of summoning change from a personal or social malaise. The grotesque, the irreconcilable, is what forces us to make up our minds.

In Shostakovich's case, the role-model was Gustav Mahler – 'Dostoyevsky retold by Chaplin' as the young composer's mentor, Ivan Sollertinsky, used to say. Like Mahler, Shostakovich became the master of a creative impulse in which the perception of an outsider could be earthed and mobilized through the manipulation of symphonic forms: a purveyor of apocalyptic frescoes, set in our time by their mortal and stylistic introspection. Mahler lived in the same world as painters such as Schiele and Klimt: Schiele with his biting candour and acid pungency of line, Klimt with the tremulously overblown and shimmering decoration that he applied to pornography.

Mahler too was fascinated by the decay of aspirations, and he was redeemed by the remorseless lucidity and intelligence with which all parts of his creative vision were pursued and refined. Style sets the agenda for the substance: its voluptuous colour, its sinuous twists of reference and idiom as a great musical tradition is celebrated, caricatured, probed. A Mahler symphony is a game: a display into which peacock's tail of stylistic genres has been subsumed, a commentary underpinned by the grotesque in its most sardonic form.

For Shostakovich, torn between turgid duties and his inner needs, this offered the only viable way ahead. Chameleons, said Shelley, feed on light and air. Shostakovich's own music is a dialogue between external circumstances and the needs of his own mercurially complex personality (that 'box of false bottoms', as a youthful confidante called it) which, left to itself, could generate enough shades of naive enchantment, moral equivocation and anguish to last a lifetime. It is the solitary game of an oppressed and unhappy man, played as much on himself as with his perception of the world outside.

It exists as code, a performance in a double sense, the product of a court-jester whose private phantoms had to be processed through the wringer of mock-heroic sublimation. In the *Second Cello Concerto*, and increasingly as his life runs out, he sets himself on a gothic stage complete with tambourines, fanfares and whirring clocks. You hear insect stridulations that seem to inhabit the same world as Bartók or Schoenberg; but they frame scenes of desolation which make their dispassion all the more sinister. The musical doodlings with which the *Eighth* or the *Fifteenth Symphonies* die away are not carefree. They hint at the crawling embarrassment, the hopelessness and estrangement, that follow an offence.

His final works open a Chinese box of acrostic and allusion. Flippant music, sometimes – in which chaos is drummed down by a sort of automaton of fatuous martial rhythms. These are the rituals that neurotics use to ward off panic, and for a few spinning moments all pretence of control is lost. 'I think this is tragic,' ventured the conductor Kurt Sanderling, at the premiere of the last symphony, as yet another brittle quotation from the *William Tell Overture* bolted past. 'You're not wrong', the composer replied. What he did not add was that the germ of the music was his childhood recollection of a toy shop, when hopes were still clean, and had yet to be disappointed.

Where can the disappointment have come from? Shostakovich's obituary in *Pravda* hailed him as a citizen-artist, 'a faithful son of the Communist Party' who 'devoted his entire life to reaffirming . . . the ideals of Socialist humanism and Internationalism'. His funeral in 1975 was broadcast live across the Warsaw Pact countries – as befitted a winner of Stalin Prizes (now expediently forgotten with the dictator's fall from grace), Honoured Artist of the Russian Federal Socialist Republic, People's Artist of the USSR, three times recipient of the Order of Lenin, Hero of Socialist Labour, Deputy of the Supreme Soviet, and more. Western classical music radio played the *Fifth Symphony* (a work so studiously accessible that their listeners might manage not to switch off), commiserating with the Empire of the Bear on its loss.

But the story was not quite over. Four years later, in 1979, either Shostakovich, or an impostor claiming a privileged audience with him in his last years, sprung upon the world *Testimony*. Claimed to be the composer's memoirs as dictated to his amanuensis, the music journalist Solomon Volkov, it was published when Volkov gained freedom in New York. 'I never tried to flatter the authorities with my music,' the new Shostakovich pronounced. 'One man has no significance in a totalitarian state. A mechanism needs only cogs. Stalin used all of us as cogs. One cog does not differ from another, and cogs can replace one another so easily. You can pick one out and say: "From today you will be a genius cog" and everyone else will consider it a genius. It doesn't matter whether it is or not. Anyone can become a genius on the orders of the leader.'

Naturally, the book was an instant *succès de scandale*. Khrennikov's visceral embarrassments, the torture of the too-brilliant theatre Director Meyerhold (and his wife stabbed in her eyes, screaming her last moments away as pedestrians scurried by) despite Shostakovich's entreaties for their lives: a withering denunciation of Lenin himself, the description of how Stalin had shot in pique his rocketry experts, leaving Leningrad next to defenceless. 'You had to take a guest into the toilet to tell him a joke. You turned on the water full blast and then whispered the gag. You even laughed, quietly, into your fist. A marvellous tradition.' It delivered the goods which, if true, made for the best autobiography since Berlioz's.

But was it true? There were no taped interviews. Shostakovich found a microphone as terrifying as a snake, said Volkov; you'd picked up what you could with shorthand. Circumspect westerners found inaccuracies and, alongside them, revelations that seemed unavailable elsewhere. There were murmurs from expatriates of how much in *Testimony* was genuine, despite all the official trophies that Shostakovich had accepted, the hack-commemorations that he had so eagerly penned. Volkov had meant to write a biography, their theory went; he might have dressed it up as autobiography for publicity and gain, but the crux of what he said was right.

Before the end of the year, a response had appeared in Moscow's *Literary Gazette*. It was endorsed by several dozen former colleagues and entitled *Pitiful Forgery – concerning the so-called Memoirs of D D Shostakovich*. Its most damning signatory was the composer's third wife, Irina, who appeared on television to say how little Volkov had known her husband, and how he had not visited the family enough to gain what he claimed. Laurel Fay, an American musicologist, discovered passages in Shostakovich's old speeches that Volkov had rehashed as if they had been written years later: these, and these alone, were what Shostakovich had been duped into signing away as authentic. And when Shostakovich's son Maxim defected to the west in 1981, he dismissed *Testimony* as a patchwork of gossip magicked from nowhere.

Yet the story's twists were not over. Gerald Abraham, a leading British authority on Soviet music, had known Shostakovich and his friends: *Testimony* was absolutely consistent, he declared, with his own understanding. Just arrived in the west were the two conductors who had premiered several of his most courageous symphonies. Kirill Kondrashin braved the *Babi Yar* debacle in 1962, whilst Rudolf Barshai (who'd arranged for orchestra Shostakovich's own memorial 'to the victims of Fascism') confessed to the *Sunday Times* of Volkov's account, 'It's all true.' Shostakovich's former pupil, the cellist Mstislav Rostropovich, explained that the symphonies were a secret and coded dissident's critique of his nation's history; and Rostislav Dubinsky – Shostakovich's friend, leader of the Borodin Quartet – affirmed that they were a portrait of the Soviets' destruction of Russian culture. Dubinsky's autobiography, *Stormy Applause*, chronicling thirty years of musical browbeating, describes how it was necessary to play the *Fourth Quartet* in two ways: often with florid smiles, only daring occasionally to bare its bitter subtext of disillusionment. One hears a canon as sweet as a nursery-rhyme, which opens seemingly illimitable possibilities – all of them observed askance, as if through a peeling mirror. Its finale, rhythmically speaking, pre-empts *A Career* in the *Babi Yar* symphony of thirteen years later: and perhaps shares with it the wearied sense of triumphant subtlety and reason. But then, Shostakovich's music was always the stuff of codification and ambiguity.

By now biographies had appeared thick and fast. Rostropovich's wife, Galina Vishnevskaya, drew on her years as the composer's intimate professional friend. 'If art can be called anti-communist, Shostakovich's music should be known by that name.' Vladimir Ashkenazy described the composer's misery when he had been forced to join the Communist Party. Most dramatic was Maxim

Shostakovich's about-face. His defection and its aftermath had been a nightmare, with KGB harassment at 1.30 in the morning ('I knew: it was now or never') and the pressure on him to vilify Volkov had been unendurable. It seemed an old tyranny had lost none of its teeth.

Marx grasped what the Jesuits had only glimpsed: that the social being of men determines their consciousness. The great philosopher envisioned the system that made Maxim's father, as well as breaking him. Dmitri agreed. 'Without the revolution, I should probably never have been a composer.' He was born in the city of the 1905 Uprising, months after the event; and one his first scores, drafted when he was ten, was *The Soldier*. 'Here the soldier fires' he writes at one point, somewhere in page upon harried page that leaves nothing to the imagination. His *Second Symphony* depicts the shooting of a Cossack boy for stealing an apple during the riots of 1917, which Shostakovich saw for himself. 'I didn't forget that boy' he said of his trauma. 'And I never will.'

'Insurrection is an art,' said Trotsky, 'and like all arts, it has its laws.' Briefly, in the years following the 1917 revolution, the Soviet Union was in the vanguard of the world's avant-garde. The poet Mayakovsky wrote of 'spitting out the past, like a bone in our throats' and Lenin was keen to foster artistic freedom, provided it served the goals of *agitprop*. An educated, westernized sensibility brought fresh sophistication to the ripe opulence of Russian folk traditions, while the pioneers of Suprematicism and Constructivism sought to hone their hard new aesthetic with a discipline and scrutiny that could encompass the horizons of a machine age: Kandinsky, Rodchenko, Malevich amongst visual artists, the films of Eisenstein, the incandescent futurism of the novelist Mayakovsky. Before the revolution, Shostakovich's own city of St Petersburg had been the home of Rimsky-Korsakov, and it was there, in 1908, that Rimsky's pupil Stravinsky had unleashed his *First Symphony*. There too, music from the west's cutting edge was performed: Reger, Mahler, Debussy, Ravel, Richard Strauss, *Les Six*. Amongst the cultural traffic between St Petersburg and the west was a festival of Russian music in Paris, organized by a young entrepreneur, Sergei Diaghilev. Following the introduction of the New Economic Policy in 1921, Bartók was feted when he came to Leningrad (as it would shortly be called) in order to play. Shostakovich had the appetite and the ears to absorb everything he heard, and as he completed his musical studies he embraced Bolshevik iconoclasm with zeal. He flirted with Constructivism, which drew its inspiration and materials from modern industry; and the sculptor Tatlin's revolutionary spiral design became the tacit emblem of Shostakovich's own works in their raucous evocations of factory life. The old conception of art, as a commodity and diversion for the privileged few, was under assault. As Rodchenko explained, 'The art of the future will not be the cosy decoration of family homes. It will be as indispensible as the 48-storey skyscrapers, mighty bridges, wireless, aeronautics and submarines which will themselves be transformed into it.' Whatever else he renounced, Shostakovich never lost faith in an artistic imperative that was biting in relevance and immediacy, as important as breathing.

Stalin became general secretary of the Communist Party in 1922, and with Lenin's death 1924, he set about creating 'socialism in one country'. Two years later the NKVD, his secret police, were in place. For a couple of years his apparatchiks had their work cut out on the economy, but then they were free to turn to everyday life. 'Art without content . . . technically skilful in form, but expressing in content the ideology of decadent bourgeoisie', was pilloried. In its place was Socialist Realism: national self-expression with a purpose (in effect, a sentimental idolatry of the proletariat) in which the symphony could regain a historical mission which, with capitalism, it had lost. In all this, the figure of Beethoven had a mighty significance. As Shostakovich wrote, 'Only Beethoven was a forerunner to the revolutionary movement. If you read his letters you will see how often he wrote to his friends that he wished to give new ideas to the public and rouse it to revolt against its masters.' But there was a deeper import for the Soviet musicologists of Shostakovich's youth. Beethoven alone had upheld 'the brotherhood of man' that the bourgeoisie had later subverted: his symphonies were the clarion-calls for an era in their monumentality and aspiration. If there was felt a need for a symphonist in Beethoven's mould to arise in the new order, it was a challenge that Shostakovich was uniquely equipped to meet.

'Cities are the only source of inspiration for a truly modern art' wrote his contemporary, Boris Pasternak. 'The living language of our time is urban.' Shostakovich was born with the sounds of St Petersburg in his ears. He served the city throughout its siege, and he was as battered as any member of Soviet society by forces beyond reason. Yet like the narrator of his *Thirteenth Symphony*, Shostakovich surmounts his life in a feat of creative and personal triumph. His themes don't often soar. More likely they are impacted and crabby, but what a compensating intensity they have. His music, filled with the sounds from the streets he knew, is as contemporary and as unflinching as the photojournalism of Weegee in New York, as sharply etched as Soviet cinema: yet the necessities of his times force open the gate to an unutterable world of the profoundest emotions. He listens to his contemporaries (his compatriots, Stravinsky and Hindemith, later Schoenberg, his friend Benjamin Britten and many others) and he learns from them. Above all, as Eric Roseberry argues, he attends diligently to his Marxist-Leninist role, using music as a simile for political evolution:

> In his 'heroic' symphonies Shostakovich, striving to express the new consciousness, applied the socio-historical principles of Hegel and Marx. Beginning with the Fourth, these works embody philosophical ideas such as the identity of opposites and the dialectic of thesis, antithesis and synthesis. At the same time, his music was never cold and abstract, but strove to express life in all its contradictory aspects. Man remained at the centre.

The theoreticians of taste must have felt sure of his allegiance. In truth, the darkness of World War Two mirrored the ambivalent twilight of the grotesque, and the need to write war music allowed the euphoric lies of Soviet life at last to crumble. From Mahler, Shostakovich knew how to juxtapose conflicting passages so that it was left to the listener to determine what was real. War then serves as a metaphor for a state of being in which optimism is the irony of failure, in which infinite variety can find a voice within implacable fatalism: and it lets free a language beyond self-affirmation, beyond rhetoric. Never do we see his current of raw and febrile ardour, the energy of a despairing dance or of uncauterized pain, more directly than in these six years.

When the war was over, Shostakovich had to find a new guise if he was to survive on the tightrope between official praise and savage public denunciation, according to how his latest work might be perceived. The paradoxical fool in Shakespeare's *King Lear* was one of his favourite characters, and he'd set verses with delight for a production of the play in 1941. It was the shattering of Lear's illusions, he recalled, that mattered. Shostakovich's affection was also evident for Mussorgsky, and he began to see himself as Mussorgsky's heir – perhaps even to the extent of escaping internal contradictions by playing the moralizing fool, as for self-defence his predecessor had so often done. Solomon Volkov proposes,

> *Whether consciously or not, Shostakovich became the second great* yurodivy *composer. The* yurodivy *is a Russian religious phenomenon – a national trait. There is no word in any other language that can precisely convey the meaning, with its many historical and cultural overtones. The* yurodivy *has the gift to see and hear what others know nothing about. But he tells the world about his insights in an intentionally paradoxical way, a code. He plays the fool, while actually being a persistent exposer of evil and injustice. The* yurodivy *is an anarchist and individualist, who in his public role breaks the commonly held 'moral' laws of behaviour and flouts conventions. But he sets strict limitations, rules and taboos for himself.*
>
> The origins of yurodstvo *go back to the fifteenth century. During all that time, the* yurodivye *could expose injustice and remain in relative safety. The authorities recognized the right of* yurodivye *to criticize and be eccentric – within limits. Their influence was immense.*

What evidence is there that this applies to Shostakovich? A passing comment by his one-time champion, the conductor Evgeni Mravinsky, and the early example set by Shostakovich's friends amongst *Oberiu*, the Leningrad Dadaists – no more. Even if we accept *Testimony* at face value, Shostakovich seems as much prone to retrospective self-justification as the rest of us. Under the spotlight he was no hero, nor even a holy fool, merely another frightened little man.

Yet as a key to opening up the music, Volkov's metaphor is perhaps more apt. He writes of Shostakovich's generation, 'New ideals could be affirmed only in reverse . . . through a screen of mockery, sarcasm and foolishness. . . . But these words did not carry a simple meaning; they had double or triple implications. In their works, street language grimaced and clowned, taking on mocking nuances. A joke was transformed into a parable, a child's ditty into a terrifying examination of the human condition.'

Hang on to your irony, the composer himself said. It was your safeguard and your future, the most precious gift you had. Like the murdered Trotsky, Shostakovich understood the mediocrity of evil. With the death of Mahler and Sibelius, he is the only twentieth century composer whose symphonies rise to the Beethoven's broad humanity: out of them all, he comes closest to Beethoven's fusion of compassion and the rigour of a master craftsman, in whose epic and sweeping compass not a note is without significance. The reason for Shostakovich's enduring fame is simple. He is the only composer of our time who squares the realities and necessities of that age with the highest ideals of the past.

Shostakovich wrote to his friend Isaac Glikman, 'If my hands were cut off, I would continue to write music with the pen between my teeth.' The sullen inner fires that drive an individual to make order out of chaos, against all odds, take on many forms. In Stalin and Shostakovich two men possessed were ready to collide: one of them a bullish puritan preoccupied with social control and the crushing of originality ('he worked into the night, like a thief' noted Shostakovich), the other an ascetic terrified of death and death's counterfeit, inertia. For Shostakovich the need to make sense was as necessary as breathing; a making good of debts, an act of atonement (for what?) endlessly to be repaid.

His compulsiveness never manifests itself in magpie wit or meticulous ceremony, as it did for Stravinsky, although both men were shrewd enough to know the potency of creative pastiche. Instead he is a figure from a Sartre novel, nauseated by the dread of imprisonment within his own frame, compelled as much as Albert Camus' Sisyphus to be a hero in dogged frustration and futility, for whom to do (endlessly, and that alone) was sufficient to be. Shostakovich is almost by himself in facing the traumas of the twentieth century, as well as the challenges that the devastation of its musical language must raise. Through him enlightenment shines, and he has made us aware of the chasm of unreason at our feet, through which sense threatens to vanish. As each of us contemplates the long night of our times, this frigid sensibility – born out of supreme awareness of creative idiom and of the dead weight of our century's unique capacity to appal – resonates in the mind after lighter gossip has ceased to speak.

# CHAPTER 2
# A PETROGRAD CHILDHOOD
## (1905–25)

- *1905 Uprising, 1917 Revolution*
- *Shostakovich's upbringing and personality*
- *He enters the Conservatoire*
- *Poverty and sickness*

S
t Petersburg is a spectral edifice, built upon swamps. 'The Venice of the Russias', travel-writers call it. Its canals and noble silhouettes, its lime trees and exquisite boulevards . . . those who have lived there perceive it differently. 'This rotten, slimy city should rise in smoke and disappear in smoke' wrote Dostoyevsky. 'The white mists of the Neva were blackened by the fog of factory chimneys,' recalled Alexander Werth, aware of the midsummer reek of hot tar and cursing carters, the 'cadaverous yellow water, the yellow snow' of icebound winters. 'An ochre city' remembered Stravinsky, of Italian architecture and teeming islands – blue and gold: stucco, marble, and 'purple-painted prostitutes, crying, "Men, give us cigarettes" '. The poet Akhmatova called it 'a sombre town on a menacing current – quiet, beclouded, austere.' It was the grandiloquent conception of a despot, Peter the Great, who envisaged at a stroke his window on the west at any cost, in money or in the ruination of human hopes. In the sinking of its great oak piles into slime, it was said that every brick, every stone, marked the life of a worker.

No matter, for a tax on everyone who worked there would recoup the cost of its megalomaniac vision. It was also the place where seven Shostakovich symphonies, two operas, three ballets and most of his quartets would have their premiere; and it fed his imagination from the earliest age with its shadows and fantasy,

its midsummer nights bloated with light, its Silver Age of literature, its unfathomable and mercurial water. Shostakovich's first
surviving music, filled with the nocturnal resonances of Rachmaninov and Medtner, Gogol and Pushkin, prefigures his lifelong
identification with the tragic figures of the past.

Russians understood well the mirage, caught between public
ostentation and the financial depredation of millions of lives and
of an empire, which their capital city embodied. Between 1900
and 1917 an old order slumped into catastrophe. Among artists,
Symbolists looked to the future with foreboding, while Futurists
advocated cultural anarchy. Scriabin, the craze of Petrograd (for
Shostakovich's city would change its name twice within a couple
of decades) revelled in decadence and mystic introspection.
Other events cut closer to the bone. Widespread violence culmi-
nated in the St Petersburg Palace Square massacre of 9 January
1905, 'Bloody Sunday', in which Tsar Nicholas II's troops slaugh-
tered peaceful demonstrators. As the bourgeoisie clung to the
remnants of their life (and Rimsky-Korsakov's opera, *Kaschei the
Immortal*, had its first performance) so, to the revulsion of the
world, battalions of workers were lined up and shot. Shostakovich's aunt Nadejda remembered,

> *They erected clumsy barricades and defended themselves with
> revolvers against the machine guns that had been hoisted on the
> belfries of cathedrals. . . . The orders from high authorities –
> 'Take no prisoners, act without mercy' – were carried out to the
> letter.*

Shostakovich's first dissenting piece, a *Funeral March to the Victims
of Revolution*, was for a memorial service in January 1918. But it
was his *Eleventh Symphony* of 1957 that commemorates the 1905
apocalypse: a jostle of proletarian songs and military fanfares,
scanning the frostbitten expanse shattered by bloodshed in what
Pasternak called 'a notorious trollop of dawn . . . that mirror of
waters.'

'I didn't spend my life as an onlooker,' said Shostakovich to
Volkov, 'but as a proletarian.' He was born on 12 September 1906,
and his father hurried back from work with delicacies for the
christening. 'Why don't you call him Dmitri?' asked the priest.
It's a good Russian name, and his father's name too.' 'But,' said

his mother Sophia, 'Jaroslav Dmitrievich sounds much better than Dmitri Dmitrievich.' The priest waved aside her objections. 'Dmitri's a good name.' So Dmitri it was.

His early life, the crabby old Shostakovich told Volkov, was insignificant. His parents had come from Siberia to St Petersburg, where in 1902 Dmitri *père* began work with the great chemist Mendeleyev. Little Dmitri remembered creeping across corridors to eavesdrop on a neighbour's string quartet. Sophia, daughter of an enlightened mine-manager, was a fine amateur pianist and her husband sang well enough to tackle Lensky in *Eugene Onegin*. Then came a child's revelation of hearing the same work at the opera-house. 'I was amazed. A new world of orchestral music was unfolded before me, a world of new colours. . . . ' And young Dmitri loved gypsy ballads: 'magical music, which helped me a great deal later when I belted away on the piano in cinemas. At least I'm not a snob.'

Volkov's ageing composer had reasons to discredit the revolutionary fervour of his youth, to issue his own belated counter-propaganda. His family, in fact, consisted of Polish radicals with several generations of subversion and exile behind it. Dmitri Boleslavich knew from his childhood the boisterous nature of the peasants, whose innate goodness alone, he believed, could save their nation. The Shostakoviches were *narodniks*, radical democrats like the rest of St Petersburg's intelligentsia, but by this time no more than that. Almost blandly their relatives campaigned for reform from the family home, until a memorable visit from the Tsarist secret police.

The atmosphere then was, as the poet Alexander Blok put it, charged with sickness, alarm, catastrophe, and disruption. An upheaval in the heart of every citizen, remembered Boris Pasternak; and Petrograd was at the centre of the unrest. This was where Lenin chose to return from exile in 1917, calling for land, bread and an end to war. Shostakovich recalled the story of how, in 1905, the Tsarists 'were carting around a mound of murdered children on a sleigh. The boys had been sitting in the trees, looking at the soldiers, and the soldiers shot them – just for fun. The dead children were smiling. They had been killed so suddenly that they hadn't had time to be frightened.' It came back to him, he said, in his *Eleventh Symphony*: 'It's about the people, who have stopped believing because the cup of evil has run over.'

Dmitri was a sickly child, frightened of outstretched hands and fire 'and corpses'. He was too weak to crush himself into the heaving trams, so he walked everywhere. His family was affluent and content, and he wandered on their estate. It was not until the age of nine that Sophia decided to give him piano lessons. Within days he was playing duets with her. By eleven he had mastered Bach's *Forty-Eight*, and began composing for himself. He changed at the piano, his parents realized: commanding and concentrated like a man twice his age, unable to concentrate on his mathematics because his head was 'full of sounds'. Nadejda remembers him reciting whole operas by ear, improvising themes about 'a snow-covered village, far away'. A couple of years later, this was how he came to meet the crippled painter Kustodiev, wheezing over his voluptuous nudes. For him Dmitri would weave extemporized dances. From him Dmitri gained his awareness of contemporary developments across the arts, the subtle eroticism of *The Nose*, as well as the fortitude to work during his own terminal disease:

> *One of Mitya's schoolfellows was the daughter of a Petrograd painter. One day she told her father that there was a boy in their class who was 'absolutely fabulous' on the piano; could she invite him home? He came to tea and was duly asked to play, which he did: Chopin, Beethoven etcetera, until the girl interrupted him, asking why did he play that old classical stuff, and begging him to play a foxtrot. Papa rebuked her, and said to young Shostakovich, 'Mitya, don't pay any attention to her. Play what you want to play.' And he continued with his sketch.*

Zoya, Mitya's sister, remembered him as a reserved boy, absent-minded, yet given to mischievous high-spirits 'until they started beating the fun out of him'. In 1915 he was enrolled in Mariya Shidlovskaya's Private Commercial School, where he remained until a move to the Gymnasium No.13 in 1918. He was a disciplined student, hard-working, who learnt how to use his tongue with caustic effect against bullies. His friend Boris Lossky thought that he resembled 'a small sparrow. He sat at the window looking blank-faced through his spectacles while his schoolmates played and amused themselves. Probably his introspection was due to his inner hearing. At the time he seemed out of place and helpless amongst the other children.' Shostakovich remembered that he'd learnt to assess his peers quickly, and to live with the disillusionment.

World War One had brought many privations, and in 1922 the family's gentle, indefatigable breadwinner was dead. But the direst event had been the Bolshevik uprising of 1917, where under Lenin's masterly direction the Red Guards had by night seized Petrograd's Winter Palace, and forced the surrender of the Kerensky government. At first the fatalities were limited, but violence grew on both sides until giant communal graves could alone accommodate the bodies. This was the civil war of 1918–21. Volkov's Shostakovich claimed hardly to remember the funerals; but others recalled his fright and his long, quiet threnody at the piano in a darkening room. The lists of 'liquidated enemies' were stuck up on theatre billboards. Both Shostakovich's *Second* and *Twelfth Symphonies* describe the murder of a Cossack boy: and the third movement of the Twelfth is entitled 'Aurora', after the cruiser whose guns had signalled the Winter Palace attack, birth of the Soviet Union.

After Shostakovich spent some time refusing to visit the pedagogue Ignatiy Gliasser ('his lectures already seemed ridiculous to me') his gifts as a composer and a pianist were noticed by Alexander Glazunov, Rimsky's successor as Director of the Petrograd Conservatoire. Shostakovich's father had agreed to smuggle him illicit alcohol from the State reserves, and Mitya was the go-between. Often, said Shostakovich, Glazunov's tutorials would become more indistinct as the great man, his mouth clamped at the nipple, would subside into a torpor. In return Glazunov became a second father, and Shostakovich's lifelong respect for an impeccable symphonic craftsman is clear. 'Glazunov spent all his time thinking about music and therefore, when he spoke about it, you remembered for life,' Shostakovich observed, fifty years after the event. 'He re-established the value of the simple word . . . and we did our best to re-create his mental processes.'

Shostakovich was harder on his memories of himself. 'I was harsh and intolerant. I liked to be treated with respect.' But these were cruel times. The highlight of the Conservatoire day, in the hardness of a winter, was the arrival of pickled cabbage. 'The cold piano keys' said Leo Arnshtam, 'singed your fingers.' When Dmitri joined in 1919, he could afford to study only part-time:

the rest of his time was taken up earning money for his family. He became a piano-player at the Bright Reel Theatre, run by Akim Volynsky for his 'little harem' of pretty dancing girls. When Shostakovich asked for wages, Volynsky stared down from a dirty collar. 'Young man, do you love Art? Great, lofty, immortal Art? The how can you talk to me about this filthy lucre?' Shostakovich repeated his anecdote at Volynsky's memorial gala, to conspicuous effect.

Hack-work, and the onset of tuberculosis, frustrated time and again progress on the work he planned for his graduation: a symphony, which he began in the spring of 1923. Through grinding toil he completed it by July 1925. Yet its debut marked it out as the most remarkable piece of its kind ever to be composed by a man of less than 20 years. In triumph it would be introduced by Glazunov to the world.

# CHAPTER 3
# A RUSSIAN ROSSINI
## (1924–36)

- ♦ *First Symphony: international triumph*
- ♦ *First betrayals – a victim of in-fighting*
- ♦ *The hesitant lover*
- ♦ *Stage music and 'Lady Macbeth'*

**M**ikhail Druskin, the Leningrad pianist, was close to Shostakovich in these years. A complex man, Druskin decided,
nervously agile yet youthfully charming, with an eye for the
ridiculous: zestful and daring, 'yet deeply arcane'. The *First
Symphony* embodied these contrasts and collisions, Druskin felt.
'It was Shostakovich's vocation to realize the concept of tragedy,
for this was how he perceived the world.' One could draw a
parallel with Dostoyevsky – particularly in the work that would
spell Shostakovich's downfall: his opera *Lady Macbeth of the Mtsensk
District*, which was written under the influence of *From the House
of the Dead*. Meanwhile 'life seethed around the young composer',
continues Druskin,

> *. . . sucking him onto its vortex. Anyone who did not experience
> those years together with Shostakovich must find it difficult to
> imagine the intensity of this whirlpool, which threw up an explosion
> of creative energy and provided the strongest impulse to artistic
> endeavour and innovation. The fresh wind of the Revolution
> revitalized the whole pattern of life, thrown up as it was on the
> open spaces of streets and squares. Youth, driven by the force of
> its tempestuous gales, avidly reached out for all that was new.*

A 'Symphony-Grotesque', Shostakovich once called the *First*. It was performed on 12 May 1926 by the Leningrad Philharmonic under its chief Conductor, Nikolai Malko, in a programme made up of new music. But the orchestra soon lost its world-weariness with student pieces when it came to this assured and fastidious manuscript. Malko protested the finale was unplayably fast, and Shostakovich, long feeling patronized by his former teachers, took pleasure in proving him wrong. He did Malko an injustice, for the conductor recalled,

> *I was amazed both by the symphony and his playing ... vibrant, individual, and the striking work of a composer with an original approach. The style was unusual; the orchestration sometimes suggested chamber music in its sound and its instrumental economy.*

Despite the griping of other Conservatoire pedagogues, 'I decided immediately to perform it.' Mitya, so nervous that he could neither eat nor sleep, was given his first ovation by the musicians: the Scherzo was encored, the audience was tumultuous. In Moscow it would be necessary to fight off the crush of students – only the symphony's dedicatee, Kvadri, got through. Malko presented the score to Bruno Walter, who brought it to the attention of the west.

It is a tremendous debut: clean and deft, tightly integrated and structured. Imagine that the spirit to be celebrated ten years later in *Peter and the Wolf* had been whisked off into some mischievous sedition of a ballet, as crisply timed as *Petruschka*, in which laconic imaginings float up and dissipate like bubbles. The facility, the assurance and musical craftiness, are all astonishing. It has the quality of a conjuring routine, decorous and capricious, with many of the resources that would serve Shostakovich well in later life, not least a natural symphonist's manipulation of interludes and anticlimax. It is the work of a composer looking back on the Indian summer of Romanticism, and forward to a brave new world in which any adventure is safe, every juxtaposition calculable: every incongruity, even, potentially a thing of grace.

Nadejda confided that much of the score was lifted from Dmitri's juvenilia. The first movement was from a fable called *The Dragonfly and the Ant*, the last from a setting of Hans Andersen. A fairytale quixoticism is preserved, but so too are wit, nostalgia, honesty and confidence, balance and restraint, contemplation, spontaneity and introverted lyricism, bristling sarcasm too – not to mention the pathos of Charlie Chaplin, which Shostakovich would have known and relished. A resemblance to Stravinsky is not fortuitous; for in him Shostakovich found reflected his own childhood observations of men as marionettes, the harried, behaviourist hero-victims of *Wozzeck* and *Pierrot Lunaire*. Tchaikovsky's lyrical ardour is in there, and the Prokofiev of the *Classical Symphony* or *Scythian Suite:* Schumann, Brahms and the *commedia dell'arte* theatricality of Vsevolod Meyerhold. Shostakovich's individualism surmounts them all, with its climaxes that consistently and deliberately break too soon, with the nervy ambivalence beneath its mask of often relentless optimism. Its best movement, a splendid opening, is perhaps the least indicative of what was to come, for the rest is Shostakovich's future in embryo. The disruptions of the *Allegretto* are those of whimsical impatience, but the finale, as Roy Blokker has shown, is about energy in the face of impending collapse.

Shostakovich had better luck here than he could find as a professional pianist. In January 1927 he entered the Chopin competition in Warsaw, and disappeared among the finalists despite the public calling out his name. It was a bitter blow, which manifests itself in his few subsequent works for the keyboard. 'I had to decide whether to be a pianist or a composer' he shrugged, thirty years later. 'With hindsight I should have been both, but . . . ' His Chopin was rigid and laconic, picked apart as if by a vulture. As a cinema pianist his jokes were so raucous that the viewers would complain he must be drunk. Not the stuff of which careers are made; but the portents for his own music, had he the sense to see them, were also ominous. The proletarianization of the arts was now in force, ostensibly for the purposes of Socialist Realism, but as a first line for the class warfare through which Stalin could increasingly manipulate and terrorize the factions of Soviet society. Both the Russian Association of Proletarian Musicians (RAPM) and its rival, the avant-garde Association of Contemporary Musicians (ACM), attacked the *First Symphony* for its allegiance to Tchaikovsky, a dated 'bourgeois individualist'. The result was a stylistic impasse, the first crisis of Shostakovich's creative life.

This was the cultural rout in which Glinka's *Ivan Susanin* was rehashed as *Hammer and Sickle*, and in which capitalism was personified dramatically as 'a monstrous blood-sucking creature. Repulsive, vast and bloated, Capitalism holds mankind enslaved in its gigantic, blood-stained clutches.' Lenin had abolished the *Proletkult* in 1920, but in the drive to collectivization it suited the propaganda wing of Stalin's Central Committee, and RAPM was reborn as a clique of untrained and semi-literate zealots who demanded that everything written before 1917 should be destroyed. Glazunov, seeing what was up, escaped to France. It was precisely the sterile nightmare that George Orwell's 1949 satire would delineate so chillingly. As a young man Shostakovich was arrogant, but he sensed he was not beyond attack. Already there had been moves to expel him from the Conservatoire because of Glazunov's patronage. His next project, a mockery of the New Economic Policy, was doomed to disaster.

Lenin inaugurated the NEP in 1921, as a means of rebuilding a shattered economy through limited free trade, and as a sop to the peasants who had been antagonized by his political coup. The boorish poet Mayaskovsky, who wrote *The Bedbug*, saw the Policy as a betrayal of Communist ideals. As Meyerhold, his play's director, said, 'That'll blow the cobwebs out of our brains!' and Mayaskovsky announced, 'Our duty is to blare like brass-throated horns in the fogs of bourgeois vulgarity.' Shostakovich's incidental music to this poster-paint assault on middle-class rapprochement was characteristic of his early style: brazen, monumental, but oddly agile with it. Although the farce's message was expediently filleted to what seemed to be the political flavours of the moment, in the strident confusion of 1929 it was bound to come to no good. Shostakovich's own family was offended by it. But then, neither composer nor director thought they were doing their job unless they antagonized as many people as possible.

And liberalism was at an end. There was a joke about 'doorbell fever': you heard a knock, they said there was a telegram, so you picked up your little suitcase. As *The Bedbug* had its premiere, Stalin began his liquidation of the kulaks across the Ukraine, of 'class-enemies' across the Union. Amidst the deportation of millions and the establishment of Gulags, 'capitalist elements' would be picked on and ruined (for this was the admitted term) 'sometimes'. Volkov's Shostakovich laughs at the way the censors banned the ghost from *Hamlet*, but the question must be asked of how staunch a Communist he was himself at this time. He seemed 'embarrassed' in interviews with western journalists, but his modernism was impeccable for an age of brutalized scientific materialism and acts of cynical, unfettered love. The show-trials of browbeaten intelligentsia were starting up; it was said that freedom, conscience and the sanctity of life were fictions. You had to be sharp or to die.

This establishes the language of the *Second Symphony* of 1927, and the *Third* of 1929. 'Errors of my youth' Shostakovich called them, and so they are; even if following the First must have seemed an impossible task. The Second was a welcome diversion from that challenge, a propaganda commission for the revolution's tenth anniversary, and ideal material for a starving composer. It is sixteen minutes of mercilessly voguish scene-painting, its climaxes reflecting not emotion but the angular cadences of declaimed speech, and opening with the glowering effects Shostakovich was to put to better use in the *Sixth*. Shostakovich said that he wanted to write a symphony in which no idea was used again: and this is a crisp sales-pitch in orchestration from a composer who has no plan or inclination to string two ideas together. Witheringly quirky and (as Prokofiev used to say of life in general) 'amusing', it inhabits the same world as that older Conservatoire colleague, and as such never escapes the predestinate grooves of a chimpanzee's tea-party. In the end a choir arrives for a rescue worthy of the Fifth Cavalry, all other options exhausted: 'Oh Lenin! You hammered resolve out of our misery, forged strength into our worn-worn hands. You taught us, Lenin, that our destiny has but a single name: Struggle!'

The half-hour *Third* is more characteristically Russian. It is an efficient and cheery storm in a propaganda teacup, best seen as a necessary orchestral rehearsal for the *Fourth*, for never again was Shostakovich to sound so lackadaisically smug. Once again, a choir pops up to give a rousing finish where otherwise there could only be a damp squib – or rather, a stylistic cul-de-sac banged up for a committee.

But the sense of tragedy incipient in much more of Shostakovich's work was as dangerous as his experimentalism. His opera *The Nose* of 1928 – anarchic, darkly frivolous and based on Gogol – is an amoral satire on humanity itself, in which a bureaucrat's detached nose, taking on a life of its own, is hunted down by frenzied townspeople. Both the nose, and its now-impotent owner (for Shostakovich develops the sexual implications with voyeuristic glee) are misunderstood and uncomprehending individuals, ripe for exploitation, pitted helplessly against the police and mass-psychosis. More to the point, the opera is a pungent critique of 1920's society: its petty officials, its intimidated press and false incriminations. Shostakovich explained innocently:

> *One has only to read this story to see that* The Nose, *as a satire on the reign of Nicholas I, is more powerful than any of Gogol's other stories. Secondly, it seemed to me that, not being a professional literary man myself, I could recast the story as an opera more easily than* Dead Souls. *Thirdly, the colourful language of* The Nose, *more expressive than Gogol's other* St Petersburg Tales, *presented more interesting problems of 'musicalizing' the text. Fourthly, it offers many interesting theatrical possibilities.*

But the reason we remember *The Nose* today is that, as Geoffrey Norris argued, 'it contained so many manifestations of an extraordinarily potent creative gift that immediately put it on a higher plane than anything else being composed in Russia at the time.' It has no precedent in his earlier music, and shows how far he has come. As Norris continued: 'He allowed the pace and character of the text to dictate the pace and character of the vocal line, adapting it to his own experimental idiom of the moment those principles of musical realism, of recitative closely allied to verbal inflection, that had been a familiar facet of Russian opera (particularly Mussorgsky's) ever since Dargomyzhsky had first mooted the idea in the 1860's with his *Kamennyi gost* – 'The Stone Guest'. Dissonant, squawking, complex and spikily animated, it has been called by Sergei Slonimsky 'brilliantly eccentric'.

Ivan Sollertinsky defended *The Nose* from its critics:

> *Shostakovich has finished with the old form of opera . . . he has shown opera composers the need for creating a new musical language, instead of drawing on the clichés of those imitators of Tchaikovsky and Korsakov . . . he has offered the most interesting musical experiments, based on rhythm and timbre alone. He is perhaps the first among Russian opera composers to make his heroes speak not in conventional arias and cantilenas but in*

> *living language, setting everyday speech to music. . . . The opera*
> *theatre is at the crossroads. The birth of Soviet opera is not far*
> *off.*

These were also the reasons why an early demise for *The Nose* was
guaranteed: irrepressible energy, caustic parody and 'formalism'.
In June 1929 an All-Russian Musical Conference in Leningrad
mustered a chorus of outrage, with RAPM delegates denouncing
its composer for his 'anti-Soviet escapism'. As Stalin liked to say,
'The cadrés decide everything.' So Shostakovich's score was lost
in an air-raid shelter until the late 1950s.

A year later, as *The Nose* opened at the Leningrad Maly Opera
to unprecedented success, Mayaskovsky shot himself. *The Bedbug*
was under attack by the *Proletkult* for its form and by the *Komoso-
mol* for its content. As colleagues recanted, Shostakovich disappeared quietly with his commission money to a Black Sea resort.
By now all the literary individualists he'd associated with had
been wiped out.

With modernism excised and art as a 'class-weapon', with the
death-camps opening their doors, everybody's business was to
smile. This was the age of informers and charlatans, of denunciations and doctrinaire barbarism that *The Bedbug* had foreseen. In
*The Last Toast* of 1934, Anna Akhmatova wrote:

> *I drink to the ruined house*
> *To the evil of my life*
> *To our shared loneliness*
> *And I drink to you -*
> *To the lie of lips that betrayed me,*
> *And to the dead-cold eyes*
> *To the coarse, brutal world, the fact*
> *That God has not saved us.*

Shostakovich had become a recluse, revealing nothing even when
he had been given vodka all night. His sole confidante was
Sollertinsky, the critic and scholar, whom he had met when both
suffered a test on Marxist–Leninism. This meant more than
Shostakovich's introduction to pub-crawls and poker. There was
unknown musical territory: the symphonies of Mahler, which
Sollertinsky challenged him to play back by ear. Reawakened,

Shostakovich released a flood of ideas. In 1932 Sollertinsky urged all Soviets to study Mahler, for he was 'closer to us than Debussy or Stravinsky, Richard Strauss or Hindemith' in his 'attempt to reach a human collective', unhindered by sensationalism or dogma. The *Fourth Symphony* would be Shostakovich's response to one man – a friend – to another – an exemplar: his farewell to the avant-garde, and first fruit of his maturity.

Shostakovich's first love was Tatyana Glivenko, a girl he had met while he was recuperating from tuberculosis in a Crimean sanatorium. That was in 1923, and she was two weeks younger than he was. In response to his mother's caution (she'd heard bad reports from his sister Mariya) he wrote:

> *Pure animal love is so vile that one doesn't need to begin to speak about it. . . . But now, supposing that a wife ceases to love her husband and gives herself to another, and that they start living together openly, despite the censorious opinions of society. There us nothing wrong in that. On the contrary, it's a good thing, as Love is truly free. . . . Love cannot last for long . . . and Mamochka, let me warn you, that if . . . I do marry, and if my wife loves another, then I won't say a word; and if she wants a divorce, I'll give it to her. . . .*

An ideology which was asking to be tested, yet Tatyana remembered, 'It was a love that endured throughout our lives.' But Shostakovich's moods fluctuated so much, and he found it so difficult to commit himself, that in February 1929 she married someone else. Shostakovich's face fell at the news. He came to Moscow to see her, and begged her to leave her husband. 'Only when I became pregnant with my first child did he accept that the relationship was over. For two months Mitya and I corresponded, and I wrote telling him that, yes, I was about to take the decision to leave my husband and to be with him. Then Mitya would answer, "But you probably love your husband more . . ." And so it continued until he informed me one day that he had got married himself – in secret. He wrote saying, "Of course, she's real fool, but I've committed myself". He was trying to call my bluff, and to provoke me to leave by giving me a fright. Maybe this is conceit on my part, but his marriage to Nina Varzar in 1932 was connected with the birth of my first child. . . . '

Sophia Shostakovich was, by all accounts, over-solicitous and interfering throughout her son's life. Maternal jealousy had ruined his chances with Tatyana, and when Sophia spotted Dmitri and Nina together before their wedding, she wept all night. Nina was a physicist from a wealthy family, who having given Mitya the children he craved for, spent much of her time living with another man. His response was that 'Shostakovich will never abandon his children' and in time, the loose ties permitted him to carry on sexual adventures of his own. But the marriage stayed warm, and affable enough until Nina's death from cancer in 1954.

Shostakovich's ballet suites show the same contempt for the bourgeoisie as his writing for Meyerhold's Young Workers' Theatre did. *The Age of Gold* (1929–32, with its first performance in October 1930) is sturdily efficient, as if Prokofiev could be hoisted on athletic supports, and rendered intermittently playful. Its cribs from *Petrushka* are shameless, but its finales – and here the music is glorious – are tense, bold. In the Soviet ballets of the 1920s and early 30s, there is a fusion of old traditions and the shock of the new, as the choreographer Fyodor Lopukhov introduced acrobatic elements. This muscularity, as much as populist dogma, was behind the profusion of ballets dedicated to sport and factory life. Oransky's *The Football Player* had opened in Moscow, and Shostakovich revelled in the anarchy and outrageous inventiveness that he was able to unleash on a music-hall world. *The Age of Gold* is a ballet after Jean Cocteau, a near-plotless parade of conflicts and stereotypes. A Soviet football team arrives in a western city at the time as an industrial exhibition, only to find its hearty endeavours thwarted by vampish prima donnas, unscrupulous police and wrongful arrests, decadent capitalists and (with a memorable sense of anticlimax) hostile hotel staff. In his programme essay Shostakovich coughs up the party line:

> *Throwing into contrast the two cultures was my main aim in the ballet. I approached this task in the following way: the west European dances breathe the spirit of depraved eroticism characteristic of contemporary bourgeois culture, but I tried to imbue the Soviet dances with the wholesome elements of sport and physical culture. I cannot imagine Soviet dances developing along any other line. I strove to write music that was not only easy to dance*

*to, but that was dramatically tense and underwent symphonic development.*

But no, it was not easy to dance to; and lashing out for its failure, Shostakovich complained, 'the choreographers completely ignored the specific requirements of the ballet.' Needless to say, the depraved numbers were the best: if only there had been more depravity. Yet there is more to *The Golden Age* than meets the eye. David Nice noted, 'To hear it is to note a precedent for the bizarre scenes of the *Fourth Symphony*. . . . In Act Three we hear not only the model for the desultory chain of short dances into which the symphony's finale deliberately lapses, but also the prototype of the astonishing first-movement explosion in which strings tear up the earth in frantic, fuguing semiquavers.' It says much for the pliability of Shostakovich's hyperactive idiom that it seems equally at home in the *Fourth Symphony* and his next ballet, *The Bolt* of 1931. This is surely the most stupefyingly futile plot ever committed to the stage: a sacked drunkard wrecks an industrial machine, and confesses after a young communist has been falsely arrested. There is a celebratory concert. If Shostakovich felt he had no alternative but to lend his support to this project, during a national hysteria in which sedition was suspected round every street corner ('We demand that saboteurs be shot!' screamed *The Worker*), his irreverence ended in disaster. The press complained that 'the military dance shows a complete ignorance of military matters' and concluded that Shostakovich should consider this 'a last warning. He should think very carefully about this conclusion.'

Now Shostakovich's score is, with its pseudo-anthems and bravura gallops, as happy and accessible as anything written in our century. How could such wit, such innocuous cheek, have enraged the arbiters of musical life? Well, he had learnt his lessons better when, in the *Thirteenth Symphony* of 1962, he quotes Yevtushenko:

> *Tsars, kings, emperors,*
> *rulers of all the world,*
> *have commanded parades*
> *but they couldn't command humour.*
> *. . . They've wanted to buy humour,*

*but he just wouldn't be bought!*
*They've wanted to kill humour,*
*but humour gave them the finger.*
*Fighting him's a tough job.*
*They've never stopped executing him.*
*His chopped-off head*
*was stuck on a soldier's pike. . . .*

Irony is inimical to social control. It is not the stuff of the imperative mood. It cannot be served up on parade or secreted for later denunciations. Now that *The Bolt* had been knocked out of the way, there was the rebel's fondness for jazz and the fox-trot to deal with. Shostakovich, for a bet with the conductor Nikolai Malko, once orchestrated Youens' *Tea for Two* in forty-five minutes flat. Malko, delighted with the dry fizz of a little winner, took to playing it as an encore. But the fox-trot had been tainted with capitalism's decadence, said the People's Commissar of Education:

*The bourgeoisie would like man to live not so much by his head as by his sexual organs. The fundamental element of the fox-trot derives from mechanization, suppressed eroticism and a desire to deaden feeling through drugs . . .*

Another cringing recrimination by Shostakovich, this time in *The Proletarian Musician*:

*I consider it a political mistake on my art to have granted Conductor Malko permission to arrange my orchestration of Tahiti Trot since Tahiti Trot, when performed without an appropriate setting, might create the impression that I am an advocate of the light genre. A proper injunction was sent by me to Conductor Malko about three months ago.*

Levity was also the charge brought against Shostakovich's *Piano Concerto*, Opus 35 (1933), which he composed for himself in a virtuoso display with the Leningrad Philharmonic. Beethoven's '*Hammerklavier*' had long been in his repertoire, and the concerto begins with a distant parody of the '*Appassionata*'. The finale has an uproarious quotation from the *Rage over a Lost Penny* as well as

Haydn's *D major Piano Sonata*. Both of Shostakovich's piano concertos are supremely Russian, for they inherit a far older tradition than Socialist Realism, and his flair for his favourite instrument shines through every bar. The First is surely his most carefree piece, with a relish for fireworks and circus. Yet I suspect that its jollified bathos and mock-heroics come from his stint at the Piccadilly Cinema. The first movement is a bouncy pastiche through which a trumpet solo announces, in stentorian tones, numerous changes of tack. The *Lento* is an affectionately lugubrious and graceful waltz which is as much like Prokofiev as anything Shostakovich wrote. The opening of the finale foreshadows the knowing innocence of the Opus 87 *Preludes* but mayhem soon wins the day, in a gleeful flurry that is quite as witty as Saint-Saëns' *Carnival of the Animals*. There are darker resonances too, for Shostakovich quotes the Austrian folk-song *Ach du lieber Augustin* – Augustin being a mythological character whose fondness for alcohol bears him through any catastrophe.

There are affinities between the concerto and the first, second and sixth of his *Preludes* Opus 34, which he had finished four days earlier. The ghosts of Scriabin and Rachmaninov are still in the background of these tiny but luxuriously quirky pieces, which are often dreamy, and always reveal the perceptive pleasure Shostakovich took in exploring the piano's lucent sonorities. In this, and in their rhythmic buoyancy, their intimate concentration and eloquent recitatives, they anticipate the greater essays of Opus 87. But often the Opus 34 set is as fine and as understated as a pastel sketch. A schism between Shostakovich's public and private face was beginning to emerge, as he kept his head down and planned his next major project: the first instalment in a projected cycle of four operas about women's lives, suggested to him by Boris Asafiev.

*Lady Macbeth of the Mtsensk District*, the fruit of twenty-six months' labour, is a work of courage and necessity. Shostakovich's own commentaries reveal how profoundly he empathized with Katerina Ismailova, its tragic heroine, who was 'on a much higher plane than those around her . . . surrounded by monsters'. Shostakovich's friend Galina Serbryakova remembered, 'Dmitri was thirsting to recreate the theme of love in a new way, a love that knew no boundaries, that was willing to perpetrate crimes inspired by the devil himself, as in Goethe's *Faust*.

Lady Macbeth attracted him because of the fierce intensity and the fascination of Katerina's imagination.' His old *Narodnik* feminism was not in doubt; but he found more tangible identification with the woman who was betrayed by all those around her. To Volkov, Shostakovich described Katerina's family as 'a quiet Russian family, who beat and poison each other . . . just a modest picture drawn from nature.' Ian MacDonald suggests that his mind might have been 'seething' with the recent case of Pavlik Morozov, a twelve-year-old boy declared a national hero for denouncing his family. This was an opera, said Shostakovich, about 'how love could have been if the world weren't full of vile things: the laws and properties and financial worries, and the police state.' He knew, as Katerina did, how boredom could corrode a mind as effectively as repression. In the event Katerina's destroyers, insinuating themselves cheaply and hypocritically upon a passionate innocent, offer us a microcosm of Stalin's empire between 1930 and 1932. As his Five-Year Plan collapsed, Socialist Realism reached new excesses of hectoring euphoria. The *Proletkult* had invented the mass-song, a crude setting of verse apostrophizing the leader and the motherland, which could be rattled off by farm-workers; and this was the age of the 'Five-Year-Plan novel', whose typical subject would be the construction of a power plant. Such was the subtlety of cultural life: a life in which the individual had been declared not only obsolete, but counter-revolutionary.

*Lady Macbeth* reinterpreted the 1865 novella by Nikolai Lestov, and it made an apt successor to *The Nose* in its lurid amorality. As Shostakovich suggested to Volkov, 'a turn of events is possible in which murder is not a crime'. Katerina has been trapped into marrying the foolish son of a brute, and is condemned to drag out her days among witless country bumpkins. As MacDonald rightly saw it, 'Longing for life-validating love, in which subject Shostakovich rates her a genius, she can realize her dream only by slaughtering her male oppressors.'

The soprano Nadejda Welter remembered her rehearsals. 'We saw for the first time that Shostakovich's restraint was only a superficial skin, and that a passionate spring of energy and dynamic creative force was bubbling underneath. . . . My heart literally stopped beating, so gripped was I by my impassioned desire to take the role of Katerina.'

The plot piles one indignity for women upon another: Katerina, wife of a rich merchant in a loveless, childless marriage, witnesses her fat cook Aksinya being molested by the farm-hands who have shoved her in a barrel. Coming to Aksinya's defence, Katerina grapples with Sergei, a famed seducer, who comes to her bedroom that night and possesses her. Unable to sleep, her father-in-law Boris sees what is happening. Katerina poisons him with mushrooms and hides his body in the cellar. She marries Sergei, but the corpse is discovered during a rummage for vodka. Katerina and Sergei are deported to Siberia: Sergei falls for a beautiful convict and the two taunt Katerina, who leaps into a lake carrying the new rival, Sonyetka, with her.

At first, thought Shostakovich, everything went well. When *Lady Macbeth* opened at the beginning of 1934, sold-out simultaneously in Moscow and Leningrad, it was acclaimed as the finest opera in depth and magnitude since Tchaikovsky's *Pique Dame*. It was unveiled to extravagant praise in New York. 'Socialism at the Met', proclaimed the headlines; and from London, Benjamin Britten wrote: 'There is a consistency of style and method throughout. The satire is biting and brilliant. It is never boring for a second.' But then, in 1936, Stalin came to a performance.

Volkov suggests that the Leader recognized himself in the corrupt police sergeant. That is, I think, too pat. Neither can we be sure how shocked party zealots might have been the sensuous tenderness with which Shostakovich depicts forbidden love. Stalin was right to be perturbed at something more subtle, more insidious. On a purely rhythmic level, think how unsettling this music is: how often imminent and cataclysmic collapse is offset only by some transient and fated struggle against circumstances, by the self-delusion of order and sense, by the imposition of corrupted force. We know that we have been undermined by something more profound than Shostakovich's frenzied depiction of physical sadism – the brooding calm of its aftermath among those who have carried out sadism: the choking, revulsed exhaustion of those who were forced to watch: the lingering contemplation of the ones who know their fate is sealed, the nightmare of the moment of extinction itself. All of these things, too, are there. It is an opera of darkening blood and the heavy aroma of blood, made more deadly by its momentum and eerie alienation, its blend of irony and grimness. If there is fulminating rhetoric, it is spared for those moments of reckoning where commentary and memory confront us. Events themselves, and the subterfuge with which they are planned, are presented with often sinister poise. To such an extent Shostakovich provides the epitaph for an era, whether consciously or by the accident of brute events that rebounded in his consciousness..

How powerfully *Lady Macbeth* sets out the agenda not only for the *Fourth Symphony* – with which it shares a metalline, frantic vitality – but for Shostakovich's career. The tramp of marching policemen reappears for the arrest of Anne Frank in the *Babi Yar* Symphony: both *Fears* and *In the Store*, from that same work, recall the labour-camp scenes of *Lady Macbeth of Mtsensk* ('Road, where the chains have been dragging, / Where the bones of the dead are still lying . . . ') The *Eighth Quartet*, dedicated to the victims of Fascism, quotes Katerina's entreaty to Sergei in Act IV: 'Seryozha! My dearest!' Truly *Lady Macbeth* bears the imprint, not only of Shostakovich's life-long identification with the victims of oppression, but of his perception of himself as underdog. As Katerina says, 'It's hard after endearments and caresses / To feel the whip on your back.' In that sense, Stalin was right to see himself as the gatecrasher at a feast about which he understood nothing. He is the spectre at the feast – and a vengeful one – for two decades of Shostakovich's life.

Now, the similarities between stage works and didactic symphonies are often overlooked. I mean the ability to paint a picture in strokes of orchestration, to think in terms of long lines and climaxes, and (like a story-teller) to wrong-foot an audience's expectations at the crucial moment. If the result of Politburo bullying is that with Shostakovich's defection we have lost one of our century's most exuberant writers for the stage, that loss is the symphony's gain. But first, we need to look more closely at the debacle that marked the turning-point in Shostakovich's wretched vocation.

Recently H.G. Wells had interviewed Stalin, and in a prophetic radio broadcast he warned that, without the toleration of criticism, Russia was bound to atrophy. 'She will slacken and stagnate again: she will breed a robot people.' What Stalin had in mind was far worse than that.

# CHAPTER 4

# THE GREAT PURGES
## (1936–45)

- Shostakovich is made 'an Enemy of the People'
- The extermination of millions
- A 'great patriotic' war
- Chamber music, Symphonies Nos.4–8

By 1936, contact with the west had been all but cut off. A stretch of Soviet territory with forty million inhabitants lay like a vast Belsen, a quarter of its people dead or dying, the rest too starved to bury their families, shamed that they were still alive. Squads of police and party officials, as well-fed as pigs from *Animal Farm*, supervised the victims. Their method had been simple: to decimate Ukrainian and Cossack national life, to set grain quotas so high that they could not be satisfied, to remove every handful of food and prevent external help from arriving. Who needed death-squads?

On 28 January, a couple of days after Stalin had been to see *Lady Macbeth*, a three-column leader appeared in *Pravda*. Entitled *Chaos instead of Music*, it continued:

> *From the first moment, the listener is shocked by a deliberately dissonant, confused stream of sound. Fragments of melody, embryonic phrases appear – only to disappear again in the din, the grinding, the screaming of petty-bourgeois innovations. This music is built on the basis of rejecting opera, on 'Leftist' confusion instead of natural, human music ... all this is coarse, primitive and vulgar. The music quacks, growls and suffocates itself. All this could end very badly. The danger of this trend to Soviet music is clear.*

It hit Shostakovich like an axe. Returning from a lavish official trip to Turkey, he became an overnight pariah, an expedient scapegoat waiting for shipment to the Arctic circle, or death. A friend wrote to Stalin, begging him to forgive the composer's degenerate aberration. But instead, the Leader went to Shostakovich's ballet *The Bright Steam*, and another attack followed ten days later. 'Now everyone knew for sure that I would be destroyed' Shostakovich remembered: the anonymous hate-mail, the abuse across streets, the newspaper announcement, 'Today there is a concert by Enemy of the People Shostakovich.' Sollertinsky alone stood by him, until a unanimous declaration of censure by the Leningrad Composers' Union scared him off. Vissarion Shebalin, attending an official denunciation at the Moscow House of Writers, declared, 'I consider that Shostakovich is the greatest genius amongst composers of this epoch.' His own music was dropped instantly, so he starved. Contemplating suicide, Shostakovich destroyed his papers and camped by the lift each night so that his family might be spared the commotion of his arrest.

In anguish he visited his protégé, the Marshal Mikhail Tukhachevsky, who promised to intercede with Stalin – unaware that his own execution was only a matter of time. But Shostakovich was reassured enough to attempt a little more work: the completion of his *Fourth Symphony*.

Ian Macdonald, taking his cue from Volkov, suggests that Stalin never intended to kill Shostakovich. The master had the mentality of a peasant, Macdonald observes, scanning files into the night to identify those people 'for whom the charisma of inspiration wove a tangible magnetism', and of whom he was in superstitious awe. No, not so. Venyamin Basner remembered that Shostakovich was drawn into the investigation of Tukachevsky's imagined plot against Stalin, and ordered by his interrogator to reappear after the weekend. He did so, bag packed, waiting for the end. 'Who have you come to see?' demanded a soldier. 'Zanchevsky.' 'He's not coming in today, so there's nobody to receive you.' Zanchevsky had himself been imprisoned the day before. To that accident we owe the existence of the *Fourth Symphony*, and everything else.

The Fourth, reconstructed from orchestral parts, had its first performance in 1961. Rehearsals were advanced when, in December 1936, Shostakovich was told by the Director of the Leningrad Philharmonic that its performance must be cancelled. The atmosphere had been electric with fear and tension at this 'formalist' adventure; and with his wife and a baby daughter to support, Shostakovich had no choice but to withdraw it for good.

That was not before its qualities had been appreciated by Otto Klemperer. In May 1936 the great German conductor turned up at Shostakovich's house, having slipped away from the Leningrad Opera. At dinner, after he'd been played the work in a piano reduction, he spoke with passion: declaring that heaven itself had granted him a marvellous gift – the chance to conduct this music on his South American tour. After a triumphant Beethoven concert the following evening, Klemperer announced that congratulations did not belong to him, but to Shostakovich and a new symphony.

Shostakovich believed that symphonic form was 'a perfect place profoundly to express different aspects of present-day life and man's attitude to it.' The Fourth was, he said, music about man and the world, about internal and external reality. It was his first fusion of monumentalism and an overriding philosophical concept. The consequence is a work at once abstract, concrete and realistic, with its marches and waltzes and Russian gallops. And in its new-found humanism, seeking to appeal to intrinsic aspects of our human condition, it is the foundation stone of the symphonies to follow. As the Soviet writer Sabinina put it:

> It would be incorrect . . . to look for links between Shostakovich and Mahler only in their language . . . the sudden and seemingly similar contrasts representing the gulf between the internal world of the artist and the aggressive banality of his surroundings. The 'Mahlerian', in the deepest sense of the word, lies in his approach to the problem of 'the individual in his surrounding world', his attempts to expose fully the contradictions in life which torment him.

Mahler led Shostakovich to question his modernist symphonic style, adopting instead a majestic scale which would allow him to create music that functioned on two levels: as a testimony of experience and as a structure that was satisfying in its own right. Finding the balance had been the bugbear of nineteenth-century Russian symphonists, but in Tchaikovsky Shostakovich discovered a composer whose finales had the form of an emotional apotheosis. It was a lesson worth remembering. The Fourth is, in fact, a calculated reappraisal of the increasingly giant structures of Mahler and Bruckner: a little central interlude framed by two immense episodes, each of them less a formal development of arguments, more an onslaught of ideas: a stream of consciousness that is both theatrical and richly experimental, an austere and unstoppable melodic continuum.

None of this does justice to the symphony's spirit. 'Grandios-omania' Shostakovich later called it – a comment that acknowledges its creative exuberance, but scarcely the balance of its craftsmanship. Automatism, the metaphor of a brute machine that might run haywire at any moment, allows a composer to play off the tension between relentless causality and anarchic indeterminism, between control and the negation of control, between rhetoric and shivering fright. You sense the audacity and excitement as Shostakovich reins in and gives form to music that threatens to fly off with a life of its own. The Fourth is dance-music in which parody and burlesque have been elevated into a mighty agent of change, with bucolic and savage elements fighting it out for supremacy over the themes that have found a foothold.

Its opening movement, an *Allegro poco moderato*, has been dismissed as a shambles. But Richard Longman has shown better, revealing how shrewdly Shostakovich creates a sense of displacement and alienation. The finale opens with a funeral march, only to twist the optimism of Mahler's *Fourth* on its head, ending in the collapse of meaning, the gaping chasms of the grotesque. Shostakovich saves the triumph of this music for its final coda; and it seems apt that, after an outburst as frenzied as a heart-attack, his exploration of the limits of a style relapses, not into a whimper, but into an interrogation of silence.

The *Fourth* is the missing link between early experiments and the symphony of 1937 upon which Shostakovich had to pin everything, if he were to salvage his future. The interplay of brutalization and reconciliation, which he had picked up from the Fourth, would be there: so too its snapping rhythms, a theme or two, and the facility with which those themes undergo magical transformation. There should be the daring leaps of the *Third Symphony*, the textures and rhythms of the Opus 40 *Cello Sonata*.

In no sense, then, is Shostakovich's *Fifth Symphony* the break with his past that it is claimed to be – and we remember that its obsequious subtitle, *A Soviet Artist's Creative Reply to Just Criticism*, was coined not by the composer but a journalist.

Yet something would be new: a Beethovenian striving and clarity of intent. Seldom has an act of expedience – least of all, desperate expedience – drawn such sincerity and transparent eloquence from those forced to carry it out, as in this meltingly compassionate work. Its surging forward movement derives from its aphoristic intensity and its bold, sweeping lines: through them both, an opening of ominous moral neutralization unfolds into a drama on a genuinely heroic scale.

The *Fifth Symphony*'s structure gives a narrative cohesion to Shostakovich's language that is accessible and uncompromised – graceful, even. The conclusion to its first movement, emotion as if witnessed by twilight, might well have come from the coda to the Fourth. But here it is the afterword to a statement, not of irony, but of almost scarifying candour. The Fifth is the most openly Mahlerian symphony of Shostakovich's in the voluptuous melancholy and welling, ineffable growth of its *Largo* – with its forlorn and pendant suspensions, its sense of levitated grief. But Mahler's voice informs more than that. Listen no further than the tremulous dialogues of the second movement, or the bitter-sweet *Ländler* of the Scherzo, to see how much it lies behind the music's command of expectations, the context within which disparate episodes work to compelling effect.

The *Fifth* is music both private and universalized: and it is made human – compared to Shostakovich's earlier symphonies – by its formal discipline and by its sense of profound disappointment. You feel them in the tightness of its phrases, the quality of its proportions. The ending has to work through the motions of a breakthrough into sunshine; or rather, into the cracker-motto optimism of a brave new world so beloved of the People's cultural hygienists. Shostakovich wondered what might have happened if he had finished in the pianissimo minor, as in the Fourth. Yet now, in his duties, he does not waver. He paces his long transition so well, and with such dignity, that the finale seems nearly inevita-ble. We might almost be forgiven for disputing Rostropovich's verdict: 'Stretched on the rack of the inquisition the victim still tries to smile in his pain. Anybody who thinks the finale is glorification, is an idiot.' But no, played at the composer's intended tempo, it is anything but glorification; and brashness triumphs over the nobility of the Largo, which had quoted the *panikhida*, the Eternal Remembrance of the Orthodox funeral. Evgeni Mravinsky, its first interpreter, was convinced that Shostakovich had tried to write an exultant finale – and baulked at it. The joy of this music lies in its ripe rhetorical ambiguities; but as Richard Taruskin has proved, a tragic sub-text was recognized soon after the appearance of a symphony that stared an unspeakable epoch in the face.

'The people recognized themselves,' said Sof'ya Khentova. At its premiere they were in tears: as the last note died, the hall exploded into a forty-minute ovation, the likes of which had not been witnessed since Tchaikovsky had conducted his *Pathétique*. A group of Party activists mounted the stage and proposed that a telegram of greeting should be sent to the composer from his audience. Higher bureaucrats were unimpressed, claiming that the audience had been hand-picked. At last, the Fifth was grudgingly auditioned by the District Party Committee and with condescension, Shostakovich was rehabilitated.

It wasn't wise for him to try and gain more favour by claiming that he was working on a Lenin Symphony. The *Sixth* (1939) is nothing of the sort, but a piece as finely crafted as it is has always been underrated. It is an act not of retrenchment but of consolidation: thinking on the same long lines as the *Fifth*, exploring with gritty strength the epic potential of Mahlerian lament; essaying symphonic form as a medium for organic structural growth, examining ambivalence and neutral emotional coloration without their becoming inert, yet somehow filling every bar with life. The first movement, which hovers like some sinister bird, is masterly in its command of pacing and atmosphere: the second is a scherzo that seems to swoop out of grey cloud, with the pummelling energy of industrialization on a superhuman scale. The finale, salvaging comedy from disarray, contemplates Rossini's *William Tell Overture* as tartly as the *Fifteenth Symphony* was to do. A buffoon-like interlude might represent the fluster that passes as meaning in futile lives and dead societies. It is, on its inscrutable surface, as jolly as the film-cartoons of 1940s Italian Fascists, and a torch song for the civil servants of any era. More to the point, the *Sixth Symphony*'s fantasy and exploration of controlled time makes possible the *Seventh* and *Eighth*. It was condoned for its genuineness, and received with utter disappointment.

Shostakovich's mind had turned to private utterances, and that most inwardly personal of genres: the string quartet. The *First Quartet* is a rigorously crafted *exercise du style*, buoyant and filled with idyllic yearning, as if the spirit of Borodin had found its way into a neoclassical lattice-work. It is fluent, untroubled and often seems unrecognizable as music by Shostakovich. But we need to look closer. Its evolving contrasts over four movements are as elegant as anything he had managed; and it quotes *St Anthony and the Fishes*, as the *Fifth Symphony* did.

His income, meanwhile, was sustained by a choking diet of film commissions, for which he received the Order of the Red Banner of Labour. But in 1940 there was the chance to rekindle his fame with chamber music on a Homeric scale: the *Piano Quintet in G minor*. It is incandescent in its memorial hope and melancholy, but impressive, above all, for its propulsive force – as if in its opening *Prelude* Bach had been given a searing edge for a new century. Its second movement is music cut back to bare sinews, from which the piano is all but absent. This variety – given the keyboard's muscular contribution to the first – contributes something to the Quintet's overwhelming gravitas; its unfolding panorama of long and supple lines spun out of reflected suffering. The *Intermezzo* is an endless trudge. The finale exploits the open diatonic intervals through which Mahler used to envelop music in buoyant euphoria. But for Shostakovich the emotions soon become more complex than that, as if optimistic resignation were the best one could hope for: 'the platitudes of credulous self-deception', as an over-eager westerner has claimed. When Shostakovich appeared in the Hall of the Conservatoire to give its first performance with the Beethoven Quartet, his audience rose to its feet; and their final ovation had the fervour of a political demonstration. Here was a piece that spoke to a nation on the brink of war.

Shostakovich volunteered for military service, but was turned down. Instead he joined the Leningrad fire brigade, and threw himself into the task of organizing concerts and writing war-songs, for the benefit of troops at the front and the people at home. Late in 1941 Leningrad's composers were evacuated, and friends saw him washing crockery in the wet snow beside a railway carriage, distraught at the loss of his things. Someone gave him a shirt. He ended up camped outside Kuibyshev, dragging urns of water across a courtyard. But at last he became relaxed and homely, and as a treat he invited colleagues to hear his latest symphony on the piano.

'The position of this symphony on the musical map of the future' smirked the English critic Ernest Newman, 'will be located between so many degrees longitude and so many degrees platitude.' Its tub-thumping credentials seemed impeccable, for as Shostakovich explained to his friend Rabinovich:

> In the peaceful development of the first movement war breaks suddenly into the peaceful life. The recapitulation is a funeral march, a deeply tragic episode, a mass requiem – the ordinary people honour the memory of their heroes. . . . Then comes a still more tragic episode: the common sorrow is followed by personal sorrow, of a mother perhaps. It is sorrow so deep that no tears are left. Further, there is another lyrical fragment expressing the apotheosis of life, sunshine . . . the end of this movement is bright and lyrical, the intimate love of man for others like himself. . . .

But this is not the interpretation of the older Shostakovich, if we accept Volkov: the symphony was a requiem, the composer stated, for the Leningrad that Stalin destroyed, and the Nazis finished off. Whatever you believe, the *Seventh* is for me a circus of the grotesque on an epic, a cinematic scale; and occasion for some of Shostakovich's blackest satire. It is a musical feat as flippant as Ravel's *Bolero* – something with which the rattling crescendo of its first movement shares a perplexing number of features, not least in the unctuously uncharacteristic orchestration. If the *Fifth Symphony* hinted at some genuine and surmounting act (whether a triumph over bad faith, over innocence, or whatever) the *Leningrad* is an essay whose premises are repeatedly and consciously overwhelmed by the leviathan pretensions of turgid, uncomprehending force. Its *Allegretto* crescendo is an act of studied disenchantment by means of the repetition of doggerel: if one instrument says it, the rest all have to tow the line. It is a travesty of a dialogue, the assembled wailings of a thousand troglodytes, scuttling about their vapid business with the simulated conviction of those, like Parsons in *Nineteen Eighty-Four*, who are impotent.

If this is meant to be propaganda music, its craftsmanship and clashing spheres of discourse are themselves an indictment of propaganda. How else can we make sense of the quotation from the *Fifth Symphony*, now muddied in frenetic bathos, or the episode of cryptic musical inertia which lies immediately before that conclusion of agitprop banality, and enough bunting to sink a Five-Year Plan? Beyond its expedient labels, seized after the embattlement of one city by people who knew nothing of Shostakovich's circumstances or his creative process, the *Leningrad's* aims are entirely abstract. At no point can the symphony's imagined programme do justice to the music's abiding subtlety and terraced layers of meaning. It makes more sense to say that Shostakovich brings Mahler's wit (his passion and incongruity and crispness of effect) to a feat of construction-work which, at its best, is as terse and as saturnine as anything by Hindemith. Throughout its opening, Shostakovich's robust humour gives a unifying and tensile mesh to music that seems as broad in its scope and measure as a landscape. The second movement is a funeral march (quizzical, jaunty, macabre) through which a sinister undertone worms its way like a parasite: the third unfolds as a recitative for strings, huge and passionate, in which more agile effects for woodwind are played off to create a consciousness, successively, of rapport and alienation.

Time and again one is struck by how lithe this music is: far more than the *Sixth*, where different episodes collided fortuitously and we were left to make whatever sense we could. The *Leningrad's* effects are, for such a large orchestra, glitteringly sharp. It is another chance for Shostakovich to flex muscles in his developing mastery of symphonic context and tempo. If he had been writing music for a film, not one movement would have the structure we hear today – and not one bar can be taken at face value. This is what Bartók grasped when he acknowledged the *Leningrad* in his own *Concerto for Orchestra*. It might not surprise us that after the end of the war, it fell into neglect. The *Leningrad* was a wordless narrative of mood-painting, suggested Blokker and Dearling before Volkov ever opened his mouth: a tale of beauty and disillusionment, earthbound and heavy-hearted, resolute yet crushed inside.

But for a while it hit a nerve across the free world. Shostakovich completed the piano performance for his friends in a state of exhaustion, elation. His audience in Moscow continued in their ovation despite an air-raid. In Leningrad soldiers fresh from the front-line stood, recalled a witness, as if staggered by their experience of the music. The score was sent on microfilm to New York, where it was conducted by Toscanini.

Later, when Shostakovich came to trust Flora Litvinova, he confided that the symphony was about Fascism, as the Fifth had been; but not only in the guise of National Socialism. Fascism was about his own country, he said, 'or any form of totalitarian regime.' No wonder, perhaps, that at the *Leningrad's* premiere, its composer shuffled on the platform as if he were about to be hanged.

There could be no such success for his *Eighth Symphony* of 1943, for there the emotions of a ruined country are naked. It has the quality of clear water. The sparse scoring, depending for much of its effect on strings alone, creates a sombre lucidity, as it did for Sibelius: an opening of luminously magnified chamber music in which the chaos of war finds its testimony in intimate and haunted reminiscence, which only later gathers up apocalyptic momentum. Shostakovich's command of pace and tension allows him to play off the disparate voices of war in an almost seamless whole: the entreaties and catatonic exhaustion of those who succumb, the horror that seems to sweep out of clean air, the frantic automatism of those fighting to save their own lives – as Wilfred Owen had said, 'an ecstasy of fumbling' – and with it all, the concatenation of bombast and pageantry that is somehow supposed to make the rest anything other than grimly futile. The clarity of Shostakovich's orchestral thinking adds a new and chilling dimension of poignancy, and his testimony ends in the counterpoint of human and musical rituals, torpid and curiously serene, that mark out a life finally and inexorably drained of meaning.

The *Eighth* is a victim's outcry, a victim's bewilderment and shivering circumlocutions, the most nihilist music that war can draw forth: war in its fluent anachronisms of morality and scale. As Stalin had noted, the death of one person is a tragedy, and the death of one million is a statistic. But war is an ideal vehicle for a grotesque composer who is also a misfit; for in it incontrovertibly, the supposed consensus of reality shatters into splinters. Never are irreconcilable worlds of meaning more violently juxtaposed. Never do protagonists justify themselves more methodically and duplicitously (to themselves as much as to others) than they do then.

Shostakovich's language is convulsive, monomaniacal. The clash of major and minor has been used since early Romanticism to generate tension, but Shostakovich uses it more explicitly than in any of his other symphonies to suggest something beyond tragedy. The result is one of his most complex and intensely satisfying structures, rich on every level, its long, implacable climaxes culminating invariably in some act of evasion, or else in the dark labyrinths of futile and coercive experience that make up the panorama of conflict.

Danil Zhitomirsky, a music journalist, remembers the Party's anger at the courageous and unpredictable individualist whom plainly it could not control, and who was feted abroad. Positive reviews were suppressed and, after an abusive Composers' Plenum, the *Eighth* was 'not recommended' for performance.

Nonetheless, Shostakovich was made Professor of Composition at the Moscow Conservatoire, Leningrad's historic rival. There the death of Sollertinsky in 1944 spurred him to write one of music's noblest memorials, the *Second Piano Trio*. It is as scant and unearthly as the music of his late period, which it seems to pre-empt: a pastiche of styles and references whose outbursts, whilst creating momentum, only seem to add to its emotional obliqueness and disorientation. And yet its cumulative effect – as so often – is a sense of tragedy, of dismay observed by a laconic witness. As Beaumarchais said, one should weep if one did not laugh. The threnodic slow movement, opening with piano chords that seem to have been slashed out of granite, speaks most directly; and its echo in the closing bars of the piece adds a wry inevitability to its sorrows. The finale itself is a joke from Gogol, or of one compelled to roll a boulder to the top of a cliff each day for the rest of his life, and watch it tumble down. It unfolds at the level of corrosive whispers, and quotes the Jewish song of death. Someone had told Shostakovich that the Nazis used to make their victims dance on their graves before execution.

The threat of having to write a *Ninth Symphony* weighed him down. Zhitomirsky remembers Shostakovich's arrival each morning in the little garden at the composers' House of Creativity. Hearing the news from Hiroshima, Zhitomirsky started to give voice to his despondency. 'Dmitri, his eyes fixed on some point overhead, quickly cut short my lamentations: "Our job is to rejoice!" '

'I have remembered this reply all my life. It conveyed a certain fatalism, but also a spark of protest. Shostakovich had developed a fatalistic attitude towards what was demanded of him, which often had an oppressing effect. But actually, in his work on the *Ninth Symphony*, he could no longer subjugate himself to this oppression.' Certainly some heroic feat was attempted; musicians heard its victorious phrases. Yet this is not what was revealed in November 1945. Instead there was a twenty-five-minute sinfonietta of considered frivolity and dispassion, elegant to the point of exasperation, with just enough dissonance to hint at the sabotage going on beneath. Often it seems scarcely more challenging than Prokofiev's *First* until an apocalyptic finale, charged with the same darkness-made-visible as the Passacaglia of the *First Violin Concerto*. Mravinsky told his players, 'I need to hear the trampling of steel-shod boots.' In its cumulative effects this is the most aberrant fancy that the most sardonic of composers ever entertained.

Now the official response was one of rage. Volkov reports Shostakovich's account of what happened when he failed to write an adoration of the Leader, complete with chorus. 'The absurdity is that Stalin watched dedications much more closely than affairs of state. Alexander Dovzhenko . . . made a documentary film during the war and somehow overlooked Stalin in some way. Stalin was livid. He called Dovzhenko in, and Beria shouted to Dovzhenko in front of Stalin, "You couldn't spare ten metres of film for our leader? Well, now you'll die like a dog!" '

'But I couldn't write an apotheosis to Stalin, I simply couldn't. I knew what I was in for.' It was time for a final showdown.

Yet Shostakovich had the ultimate word on *Pravda* through *Pravda*, when in 1974 he commented, 'The desire to avoid, at any cost, everything controversial can transform young composers into young old men'. If friends are to be believed, his private reflections were more forthright:

> *Illusions die gradually – even when it seems that it happened suddenly, instantaneously: that you wake up one fine day and you have no more illusions. It isn't like that at all. The withering away of illusions is a long and dreary process, like a toothache. But*

*you can pull out a tooth. Illusions, dead, continue to rot within us. And stink. And you can't escape them. I carry mine around with me all the time.*

As Stravinsky used to say, Soviet composers could not afford the luxury of integrity. As Pushkin used to say: 'Kiss but spit.'

# CHAPTER 5
# PUBLIC FACE, PRIVATE ISOLATION
## (1946–53)

- *Ninth Symphony: the final showdown, the last betrayals*
- *A suppressed masterpiece – the First Violin Concerto*
- *Preludes and Fugues: critics and defenders*
- *'From Jewish Folk Poetry' – a secret outcry*

With the return of peace, it was time for the Party to re-establish its moral high ground, and crush the national introspection that the war had made possible. Akhmatova was humiliated in public for her displays of private emotion, which it was suggested were part of a plot to corrupt the young. A middle-aged satirist, who had suggested that life in a zoo was preferable to Leningrad, was also purged.

The architect of Stalin's assault on the intelligentsia was his right-hand man, Andrei Zhdanov – the same ideologue who had decided, during the recent siege of Leningrad, to let civilians starve so that his troops could be fed. Zhdanov was, in the words of Eric Roseberry, 'an articulate spokesman in framing his chosen victims, formulating policy and presiding over its implementation. He could manipulate the cultural bureaucracy with cunning, and display an extremely plausible knowledge of what was going on.' With the beginnings of the Cold War, and in 1947 the thirtieth anniversary of the revolution for which there had been no adequate musical commemoration, there was an ideology to be kept up. More to the point, there was a pretext for renewed repression. And so came the *Zhdanovschina*, which lasted until Stalin's death.

This is how pettily it turned against Shostakovich. Muran-deli, a second-rate composer, had written an opera called *The Great Friendship*, just to please Stalin. The plot had ideology, it had native dances and Caucasians. The trouble was that Murandeli had confused Stalin's ethnic group: he was an Ossetian, and the hero on stage was a man whom he had driven to suicide. Rage. But the fault was Shostakovich's really, for writing the tuneless *Lady Macbeth*, which had served as a role model. Murandeli re-canted, and said as much by turning on the composer who had taught him his wretched formalist ways.

In February 1948 there was convened a three-day composers' Plenum in which Shostakovich, Prokofiev and Khatchaturian were ripped to shreds. Speech followed speech, and the *Eighth Symphony* was singled out as 'repulsive . . . an injury . . . a musical gas chamber.' This time Shostakovich was made to crawl. The conference would not adjourn until he had been rooted out from hiding and spoken of 'my many failures, even though, throughout my composer's career, I have always thought of the People, of my listeners, of those who reared me. . . . ' In private he wrote the cantata *Rayok*, a parody of his accusers' illiterate pronunciation.

'I read' he remembered in habitual self-disgust, 'like the most paltry wretch, a parasite, a puppet, a cut-out paper doll on a string!' His wife saw him close to suicide but again, new work gave him the will to live. From now he divided his music into three categories: serious pieces 'for the desk drawer', where they should be safe from censure, occasional music such as his oratorio *The Song of the Forests*, which would one day rehabilitate him as a socialist composer; and lastly the film scores that might keep his family from starvation as his honours and opportunities were stripped away. Friends remembered him begging for a spoonful of jam, and hack-work exhausted him. 'I feel like throwing up,' he said, after finishing *Meeting on the Elbe*. But in 1947 Shostak-ovich had met the violinist David Oistrakh in Prague, and there was the finale of Oistrakh's commission to finish.

Shostakovich's *First* is one of the great violin concertos of any century: shimmering and haunted music in which not a note is too much, not one effect is less than ideally calculated. It is to his concertos what the *Tenth* is to his symphonies – pellucid in its thinking and planning, as bleak as survival in a frozen landscape, gripping in its command of dramatic inevitability. It is, I think, proof that the grotesque can achieve beauty; although the point might be made that Shostakovich's language in the two slow movements is so self-contained that his need to enlarge it elsewhere for virtuoso convention could be nothing other than grotesque in its consequences – a necessity that the composer twists to satisfying effect in a diabolical *perpetuum mobile* of a finale, filled with the cavernous (and ambivalent) medieval resonances of a tonal Fifth. But at the heart of this concerto is a magnificent and passionate passacaglia (that is to say, a series of variations on a throbbing orchestral bass-line), which swells in its possessed intensity from gloom to anguish and remembrance. It is an emotional transition whose compactness and depth are almost worthy of Mozart's *G minor Quintet*. Oistrakh asked for mercy. 'Dmitri Dmitrievich, please consider letting the orchestra take over the first eight bars of the finale and give me a break. Then at least I can wipe the sweat off my brow.'

After the 1947 Plenum, Oistrakh dropped the concerto as if it had stung him, so away it went to the desk-drawer. A *Third Quartet* slipped into performance for the Beethoven Quartet in 1946, before Zhdanov's act of attrition, and it had been more innocuous anyway. From its mischievous opening, which seems as innocent as a child spinning a top, it plunges us deep into Shostakovich's world: probing, mordant and elegantly counterpointed. It is an act of transgression accomplished through increasing rhythmic complexity – in which the *Allegro non troppo* third movement anticipates the frenetic *Dies Irae* of the *Tenth Symphony*. The Quartet's tonal intervals, too, open up from their tight cocoon to dimensions which seem conceived on an orchestral scale, through which envelopes of childlike simplicity recur as a prelude to moments of crisis. In the end, everything is resolved with a wry smile.

The careerists among Shostakovich's Conservatoire students took to denouncing him, but soon he was removed from their attention, and from his post. His music almost vanished, but a few colleagues stood by him. Sviatoslav Richter was one. Another was Tatyana Nikolayeva, whom Shostakovich had heard playing the *Well-Tempered Clavier* at a Leipzig piano competition. For her he composed his *Twenty-Four Preludes and Fugues*, Opus 87: one a day, beginning in October 1950. The cycle was, she recalled, 'a work of great depth, of unsurpassed mastery and greatness . . . a new word in polyphony.' As the party zealots sneered at his 'irrele-vance' throughout its Leningrad premiere Mariya Yudina, another pianist, declared it worthy to stand alongside Bach himself.

But the Preludes are more than an act of homage by one master craftsman for another. They are Bach reconsidered for the great keyboards of the twentieth century, whose sonorities, am-plitude and colour, Bach could not conceive. Their moods change from melting compassion (the C charp minor fugue) to grandeur (D minor) and self-parody (the D flat major fugue), grief and drama (E flat minor), a cumulative oratory as powerful as Bach's (B minor, the F sharp minor Fugue), a formidable passacaglia (G sharp major): wistfulness (F sharp minor, F minor) and a phan-tasmal undertone; almost unbearable tenderness (B flat minor, E minor, F major), idyllic simplicity (F sharp major, D major) and music that can only be described as having the brightness, the evanescence and transparency, of spring rain (A minor, A major, B flat major). This is writing of heroic strength and harmonic sophistication, which summons too a Baroque purity of tone to fire the memory of sadness into this strange, noctilucent inten-sity: to advance humour to a new level, a fused totality of expres-sion. It is music that surmounts emotion, although it leaves an abiding sense of melancholy. Just as the genesis of Schubert's great quartet movements can be found in his songs and German dances, so here is the microcosm of Shostakovich's world: the *Tenth Symphony*'s transfiguration into light, the penumbral shivers of the last chamber music. Through its overlapping strands and volatile shifts of nuance, the most secret and immense musical circumstances are aligned.

As Stalin's daughter Svetlana Alliluyeva has testified, the Zhdanovshchina made possible the virtual destruction of Soviet Jewish culture. The capitulation of Russian music to Zhdanov came a day after the murder of a Jewish actor, Salomon Mikhoels, on Stalin's orders. Returning from his conference, Shostakovich told Mikhoels' gathering relatives, 'I wish I were in his place.' This was the moment, at which any identification with the Jewish community was fraught with peril, that Shostakovich began his Opus 79 song cycle, *From Jewish Folk Poetry*. In 1963, fresh from the *Babi Yar Symphony*, he would rearrange it for soloists and the Gorky Philharmonic. The wailing of a large orchestra and of voices together, certainly, generates music of more desperate sensuality than a piano accompaniment can. The motivation stays the same: for the wiping out of a racial tradition serves as a metaphor for the extinction of individuality. Yet Jewish cultural identity means more than that to Shostakovich, really. A spiritual legacy becomes a source of liberation, and it offers a variety of personas that allow him to say what cannot otherwise be said: a coded language of dissent, richly equivocal. By the time the cycle was finished even the compilers of its songs were under arrest, and disillusionment had turned to panic.

Joachim Braun has done much to reveal what lay behind Shostakovich's choices as he set these overwhelmingly tragic poems, with their dead infants and deserted fathers, their allusions to life's accustomed poverty and loneliness. They speak in the hints and ironies of Yiddish, with their innuendoes about Siberia and 'the Star' (of David, and as used by both Nazis and Stalin), however optimistic the language in which such references are veiled. From Mussorgsky Shostakovich had discovered the Yiddish tradition of 'musicalized speech' and his settings alienate even the happiest songs, hinting at grief behind. The cry, 'Drive out the old Jew!' is set to a waltz, and evil is summoned through scorn and parody. Shostakovich was aware of what Braun calls the Eastern European Jewish 'extrapolation of mood', where gaiety changes into an ecstatic and self-obsessed automatism (listen to Numbers 4 and 7), lyricism into an act of catharsis bordering on tragedy (1 and 8), and advice concludes in deliriously whispered warning (as in the fifth song). At last Shostakovich's tonal instability reminds us how ephemeral joy must be.

There was no chance of publishing the cycle, and even at its first performance in 1955 a shiver of excitement and fear ran through the hall. Meanwhile there had been a new role for the supreme parodist: he was sent abroad as a cultural ambassador to deliver Soviet propaganda, in a state of misery that was palpable to all who met him. These were the occasions of his visits to the USA (1949), Warsaw (1950) and Vienna (1952). The good news was that the American trip forced the reinstatement of his music in Russia. When Stalin rang him, Shostakovich pointed out that all his symphonies were played in the west, whereas at home they were proscribed by order of the State Commission for Repertoire. How was he to behave, if he were questioned? 'Banned by whom?' Stalin asked. 'We didn't give that order.' And so it was revoked.

Mstislav Rostropovich was there to witness the limbo that endured until Stalin's death. 'For Shostakovich it was a calamity that the people for whom he had written his works with his very blood, to whom he had exposed his very soul, did not understand him. Each person who remained near to him and still openly demonstrated affection towards him was as precious as a diamond.' His friends remember his speaking out for victims of injustice, begging for their rehabilitation, yet urging those who knew him to defend their own interests rather than his. Isaak Schwartz recalls being ticked off by Shostakovich when Schwartz threatened to leave the Conservatoire rather than denounce the man who was his teacher. ' "I am most displeased by your behaviour. You had no right to act like that. You have a family, a wife, small children. You should think about them, and not about me. If I am criticized, then let them criticize me – that's my affair." But I saw in Shostakovich's eyes such a penetrating look of sympathy and affection for me, and such compassion!'

# CHAPTER 6
# THE PHONEY THAW
## (1953–66)

- ◆ Death of Stalin
- ◆ Symphonies 10–13: 'sunrise on the future'
- ◆ A lonely, helpless man
- ◆ A communist Composer Laureate

On 5 March 1953, as the Supreme Soviet's announcement put it, Comrade Stalin's heart ceased to beat. His stroke had come four days before, but the minions were so frightened that they left him to stew. 'Stalin's name is boundlessly dear to our party, to the Soviet people and to the workers of the whole world' the statement continued. In fact, his death was so well-timed that an assassination was suspected. Even in 1952 *Pravda* had appealed for an end to an empire's stagnation: there were still too many relics of the capitalists for boundless euphoria. 'We need not fear showing up our shortcomings and difficulties. We need Gogols and Schedrins.' With the execution of Stalin's Chief of Police in December 1953, an era of liberalization was certain. By such irony did life in the Union proceed.

Shostakovich had a sanguine attitude to thaws. Enjoy them while they last, he said to Flora Litvinova, for there are always hard winters to follow. For now, nine Jewish doctors accused of plotting to poison the Kremlin had been released, and the press demanded individuality from creative artists. 'Everyone started singing' wrote Edward Crankshaw. 'At first tentatively, then in a rush, a full dawn chorus.' Hastily Shostakovich published his *Fifth Quartet*, which prefigures the mightiest, most universal of his orchestral works – and that too was on its way.

By 1954 and the emergence of Krushchev, the permafrost was

back. But during that brief renaissance had come the first performance of the *Tenth Symphony*. Its first movement had been started, with the *Preludes and Fugues*, in 1951. As Roy Blokker says, 'Here is the heart of Shostakovich. He opens his soul to the world, revealing its tragedy and profundity, but also its resilience and strength.' The composer explained, 'I wanted to portray human emotions and passions.'

He does more than that. The *Tenth* is the least psychological of his mature symphonies, and because of it, the most psychologically satisfying of them all. In it the suave domain of the *First* is spun on its head, and lost for good. The craving for self-expression, pent up for years, the long gestation of a symphony in which every gesture has been balanced and moulded to perfection, engenders more than the climax to one of the most satisfying trilogies in the symphonic literature of any age.

The *Tenth* is the summation of the war and post-war epoch on the emotional plane of one individual, which then surmounts the vision of that period. It is, as Shostakovich's colleague Kabalevsky recognized, 'the sunrise on the future'. The dark orchestral colouring is nothing to be surprised at, nor are the sentiments which the *Tenth* seems to explore. What is new is the expressive control and self-sufficiency: trauma distanced, proportioned, crafted. The brute immediacy of emotional sensation (a form of propaganda, if not for the State, then for oneself) has been replaced by the immediacy of an artistic occasion, a need to sum up and make sense, whose richness depends on its synthesis of living and remembered elements. You might say that the *Tenth* is in part about shock tactics, about the echoes of lost meaning within an overwhelming sense of grief; and at last one mind's triumphant imprimatur, 'I alone make sense of this.'

Yet the music is too deep, too lean and compact, too richly integrated for a programmatic interpretation to be more than a sideline, almost an insult. How marvellously the rolling wave of its first movement opens out. Rhythmically the opening is hesitant, so that the clarinet's first subject comes as a resolution of uncertainties, which is then pressed into alarming new dimensions. This foreshadowing creates the symphony's sense of adventure within fatalistic inevitability. The weight of uncertainty lies heavily upon it, yet so too does the awareness of pre-ordination by a higher power. As if they were shifting veils, possibilities are opened and closed, only to be wrenched apart in an act of cataclysmic fright; Shostakovich's skill serves as a meticulous, contemptuous metaphor for the arbitrary wastage of a nation.

Or does it? His challenge to audiences was the same as Chopin's: 'Let them listen and guess for themselves'. If you wonder whether Shostakovich might have been a closet Bolshevik, recall his comments to Litvinova about a Spanish contemporary: 'Picasso, that bastard, hails Soviet power and our communist system at a time when his followers here are persecuted, hounded, and not allowed to work. All right, I'm a bastard too: a coward and all the rest, but I'm living in a prison with my children to be frightened for.' No, there is no shortage of quasi-musical interpretations for the *Tenth*. Its demonic *Allegro* is a portrait of Stalin, claims Volkov, and Galina Vishnevskaya has called this symphony 'a composer's testament of misery, forever damning the tyrant.' Perhaps it is; yet we have to be aware of a process of mythologizing on behalf of an artist who cannot answer back, and which is just as crass as anything from the Soviet era. Shostakovich was a complex, a troubled and guilty man; but as a composer he is too great to need the notoriety of those who could only find fame as dissidents. Something of the greatness of the *Tenth*, as Robert Dearling has shown, lies in the way it holds its power in reserve, its magnificent ambiguities. He writes of the first movement's crisis, 'the climactic peak is maintained with miraculous feats of scoring over nearly a hundred bars of moderate tempo. It illustrates yet again the composer's ability to think in terms of immense, cogently-organized paragraphs over vast time-scales.'

One enigma stands beyond the rest. It involves the monogram which appears when we transcribe the initials DSCH into German musical notation: D, E flat, C and B. It sounds a threat, suggests Dearling, heard even in isolation: a pathos and ambivalence which seem to embody the nature of so much in Shostakovich's music. It is the signature which appears in the *Tenth*, and in the crucial moments of piece after piece thereafter; placing Shostakovich in the cryptographic tradition of Bach, Berg and Schumann's march against the Philistines. But what can it mean? Come to think of the *Tenth*, what are we to make of the *Allegretto*'s toy-shop incongruities, which his friend Marina Sabinina interpreted as the cringing of one who sees himself as a puppet on a string? And if this is the truth behind the third movement, what do we make of its remonstrative horn-calls – summoned as if from *The Song of the Earth*, which themselves form the letters of Elmira Nazirova's first name? What have we to say about the *Moderato*'s allusions to both the embattled *Eighth Symphony* and Liszt's *Faust*?

That Stalinesque scherzo, as David Fanning has revealed, is key to the rest. It unlocks the secrets of the finale, where the DSCH monogram appears in moments of a white heat of defiance. But there, too, rhythms from the scherzo re-emerge, as does its last firework glissando, shooting up at vital stages and undermining the apparent good cheer of Soviet man at peace with himself. The first of these markers occurs halfway through the last movement, when Shostakovich veers away from one kind of structure (an untroubled sonata rondo) to a crisis-orientated sonata-form, and we suspect that something is gravely amiss.

At the end of the symphony, to clinch a rousing coda which has already driven it home, the DSCH musical signature echoes over and over again. A victory is up for grabs, but on whose terms? Is the triumph one over decades of abomination, or over oneself: the retreat into the moribund quiescence described in *Nineteen Eighty-Four*? Rumours cannot enlighten us here. The point is that the finale is complex – more so than its bemused Soviet critics ever grasped. The incursions of the Scherzo are not externally imposed conflicts, brought in to heighten the drama or salvage a scrap of unity, but an inevitable result of the finale's suppressing of its profound introduction by a flippant main theme. If you like, these quotations highlight the suspense which has arisen from a strategically-placed flouting of symphonic decorum: of one rule after another by which an epic piece of music is supposed to be written. We sense the hand of a master, whose command of form and formality is sufficient to fight them on their terms, and burn provincial Socialist Realism up in the friction.

Thousands of words have been written on the first movement, that great engine in which an episode of terror is let loose and the warnings revisited, to create a winding-down that is both subtle and sinister in its iron command. The consequence is a musical structure that rears up like two great arches – whose substance is as tightly woven, and as gripping, as barbed wire. It re-invents sonata form by taking every potential weakness of long symphonic writing and turning it into strength.

No wonder we leave the symphony feeling as if we have been

witnesses to an offence as big as human experience. Fanning concludes: 'The *Tenth* dares to expand the first movement's terms of reference by including externalized depiction in the scherzo, graphic self-assertion in the third movement, and ambivalent self-denial in the finale. Such expansion may endanger unity, such expansion may question universality; but it is precisely this endangering – this questioning and penetration to the far side of our assumptions about the symphonic medium – which seals the greatness of this work.' Eric Roseberry agrees. He implies that Shostakovich's symphonies are acts of transformation, battered by repetition and *idées fixes*, in which the rational and the ardently human, the collective outlook and the individual consciousness, take arms in the same arena. Shostakovich becomes 'the equal of Sibelius (whose concision he could rival) and Mahler (whose expansiveness without loss of tension he could command).' Could Hegel have imagined what he'd make possible?

'It seems', observed Boris Yarusotvsky at the time, 'as if the hero of this symphony has to meet the forces of evil alone.' A black mark there. In Moscow there was a three-day conference on the *Tenth*, in which friends and faintly-praising rivals fought it out; Khrennikov, inevitably, preferred *The Song of the Forests*. Abroad the symphony became a *cause célèbre*, one of the glories of the age. At any rate, its author was made 'People's Artist of the Soviet Union' in the summer of 1954. An immense apartment was arranged in which he could be interviewed by New York journalists, as if it belonged to him.

Nina died on 4 December. 'If only you knew' said Shostakovich, 'how hard my life is now.' He left his son and daughter's upbringing to the maid, Marya, concerned that his lonely distress would rub off on them. Each evening he drowned his sorrows in vodka, and found himself unable to compose. The flat was in chaos. He confided to Flora Litvinova, 'You know, by nature I'm incapable of frivolous liaisons with a woman. I need a wife, to live with me and be at my side.' In 1956 he found a Party member, Margarita Kainova, hovering over him, and settled on her – ignorant as she was of art, 'unattractive and uncharming', unloved by Dmitri and unable to understand him, but perhaps able to bring two adolescent step-children into line. The marriage collapsed in 1959. He found happiness in 1962 with Irina Suprinskaya, a lively and intelligent literary editor who was young enough to be his granddaughter, and who nursed him through his final illness.

A morbid, clinging love for his children was his way of making sense in the intervening years. He lived in constant fear that some misfortune would befall them, and he spent his time feeding them up with cakes, getting them new cars and homes, pulling strings to win them careers that others whispered were beyond their talent. His memorial to Nina was his *Seventh Quartet*, a meditation of six years later on the events of a life and a death, which we must consider for its impact on the music of the C minor, Opus 110, that most famous of all his chamber works. During his sickness after Nina's death – and his mother's, a double blow – he had written a *Sixth Quartet* in 1956. Apart from an ethereal slow movement it is strangely carefree and non-committal, but the *Seventh* was one of his favourites.

He gained some solace from Oistrakh's triumphant advocacy of the *Violin Concerto* in 1955. Oistrakh said that he lived for this music. In Carnegie Hall the conductor, Mitropoulos, held up the score 'towards the audience, as if to let the new work share in the ovation accorded to a masterful performance.' In Leningrad, following a delirious reception, Shostakovich treated his friends to a feast of stale pies (which he had bought on the street and which were as hard as stones), inedible green apples, and vodka served from plastic mugs which someone had found in the bathroom. He paced up and down: toasting the ladies, tripping over his carpet, and muttering again and again, 'I am so glad, so happy. I'm so utterly, utterly happy.' Suddenly he collapsed onto the bed in the alcove. In a childishly helpless, plaintive voice he said, 'And now all of you please go away. I am terribly tired. I want to sleep, to sleep.' It turned out that Oistrakh had arranged a near-banquet, but Shostakovich was too drained to get up.

By the late fifties he was, in effect, the Soviet Union's composer laureate: tacitly acknowledged as its greatest creative artist. He knew the fragility of pedestals. *Lady Macbeth* was in disgrace until an unpublicized performance in 1963 swept its opponents away, and much else was untouchable. In the last days of Stalin a sociologist had been dispatched to Shostakovich's flat, to give him a crash-course in Marxist-Leninism. A miracle, contemplated the scientist, that our great leader, who controlled half the world, found time to ring a mere composer. Did this composer know what he was, by Stalin's side? 'A worm, a mere worm!' wailed Shostakovich, in ironic self-abasement. 'That's right,' the half-wit concluded. 'A worm is what you are. But at least you know your place.'

Teaching, film-scores and jobbing propaganda-pieces continued to pay the bills. Why must we condemn such things? If we are not prepared to censure Samuel Wesley for his hymns, or Parry for writing *Jerusalem* (a song he would come to want to destroy, however much we revere it now), why are the west's cosy custodians of value ready to dismiss Shostakovich for his official duties, which in a secular State had the same function?

'In this situation,' as Russians say, 'genius and mediocrity are equally helpless.' Every composer has had to write his fair share of doggerel: to honour debts, to curry favour from those who controlled his future, to create the miscalculations and experiments from which he could learn. If only westerners' aberrations were as well-crafted as Shostakovich's, which were written in half the time and probably with half the conviction. And if fifty bars in a major key are the price of food and an audience for the three movements that have gone before, is that really so bad? At least cinema music has brought us *The Gadfly* of 1955, which depicts the struggles of the Italian people under Austrian occupation. Shostakovich's idiom is nostalgically sumptuous, reminiscent of Respighi and above all Tchaikovsky, so that the graceful *Romance* deserves its fame.

This finesse shines through the second of Shostakovich's piano concertos, which he wrote in 1957 as a birthday present for his son Maxim. It works on many more levels than the First did; but again, Shostakovich seems to be as happy in his music-making as he ever was. He sees the piano as a percussive instrument, lending itself to contrapuntalism, as well it might in a concerto of such neoclassical panache. This time there are no worthy Soviet histrionics, for all that survives from Shostakovich's cultural background is that indispensable, bravura motive force. Beyond it, the prevailing sense is of quirky wit, the spontaneous lightness of touch that breathes life into Bartók and Ravel's late concertos, yet touched in its slow movement by the melting plangency of Rachmaninov. It tends to be sanitized horribly today, but in the composer's own recording the piano in the first movement at least comes up like a tiger – and we are reminded of what a clout to the ears his music could be. Later Dmitri dismissed the *Second* as being 'without merit'.

Briefly, it seemed a good time to be alive. On 25 February 1956 Krushchev, now Party Leader, delivered to the Twentieth Conference a historic denunciation of Stalin. It turned out that between 1937–38 seventy percent of Central Committee members had been shot, that anyone differing from Stalin was 'doomed to removal and to subsequent moral and physical annihilation.' Krushchev spoke of the 'accumulation of immense and unlimited power in the hands of one person', the tortures and false confessions, the liquidation of experts that had almost cost Russia the war. No wonder his speech was only fit for a closed session. But over the next two years several million political prisoners would be released, and the Shostakovich flat became like a small hotel for those on their way back home.

In spring air, the incandescence of early revolutionary days was often recalled. There was a revival of 'revolutionary romanticism' and these were the circumstances in which Shostakovich wrote his *Eleventh* and *Twelfth Symphonies*. The first of them is dedicated to the abortive revolution of 1905. To western ears it is an hour's worth of musical knitting: atmospheric perhaps, but as an individual statement nowhere approaching the league of the *Tenth*. The trouble is that the devil always had the best tunes – at least for Shostakovich he did; and in the prolix first movement ('The Palace Square') what we seem to catch is a composer stuck under a spotlight, chafed by his starched collar, doing dutiful worship at the shrine.

Yet our notion of the artist standing alone above society, rather than being at one with his people, is a modern intellectual conceit. The origins of art lie in the humanity of common experience. The carnage of 1905 Shostakovich had seen with his own eyes, and his need to communicate his testimony in accessible terms, was sincere. At its best the symphony draws from him the most idiomatically Russian music he could write: rolling like a great wave in the *Allegro* ('January the Ninth'), which has been aptly compared to a mighty tracking-shot. For if the *Eleventh* is a poster rather than an essay, it is a poster for a feat of gargantuan cinema too big for images, superior in some ways to the famous *Leningrad*, paving the way for the scale and the musical world of *Babi Yar*. The third movement quotes a popular song, 'You fell as victims', in an evocation of eternal remembrance as poignant as Mussorgsky. It may be that we, with our liberal sensibilities, prefer *Babi Yar's* final appeal to personal freedom to the *Eleventh Symphony's 'Tocsin'*, where the souls of the dead rise up to accuse – but we do so thanks to our own ideological preconceptions, for each has its zeal and its message.

An eminent politician on a trip to Moscow described the premiere. 'The whole of a huge crowded hall was seething with excitement. Whether he wanted to or not, the composer of this magnificent revolutionary work had to go on stage and accept the applause. But the Soviet people honoured him justly as a man who had enriched their culture and the culture of mankind with an undying work of art.' If only its real significance had been known. Lev Lebedinsky, aware that the symphony was composed in the aftermath of the Hungarian Uprising, draws attention to the quotations from revolutionary songs, which 'refer unequivocally to the tyrant's black conscience and the horrors of prison.' 'Papa, what if they hang you for this?' asked Maxim at a rehearsal. The *Eleventh* is the statement of a modern Aesop who had said of Solzhenitsyn's *One Day in the Life of Ivan Denisovich*, 'It's reality varnished over. The truth was ten times worse than that.'

The *First Cello Concerto* too has a crafty line in quotations, including one from Stalin's favourite song, *Suliko*. It was inspired by Rostropovich's performance of the Prokofiev *Symphony-Concertante*. Rostropovich received his dedication on the evening of 2 August 1959, and learnt it in four days.

Both of Shostakovich's cello concertos put to use a certain weight of crumbling rhetoric, and chart its decay through nagging obsessionality to extinction. The *First* is music that dances as if in the face of suffering. Its opening is ascetic yet possessed of vehement pace: the *Moderato* slow movement is lithe and breathlessly poised, using the cello's colours and harmonics to create an effect as disembodied as a crime heard in the night. A long cadenza soars above its sombre horizon and – as in the *First Violin Concerto* – a soloist's private world is pulled to shreds by the orchestra's febrile disorder. In this way, just as before, an individual is swept up in collective hysteria for the finale. A final self-quotation lets us glimpse the composer's sardonic mask, as if he were saying, 'I told you, all this was bound to happen.'

The first movement's tension derives from the contrast

between the kinetic force of a true sonata allegro, and the repetition of its material. It is as static as a treadmill. Self-mocking but serious, sparse yet ripely expressive, pessimistic and vital, this is one of Shostakovich's boldest and most idiosyncratic creations. Like Gogol, he stands self-absorbed in front of a mirror, reciting his own name in alienation and disgust.

In 1960 Shostakovich was re-appointed to the post of First Secretary to the RSFSR Composers' Union, a position that required membership of the Communist Party. Why did he acquiesce? Out of fear for his children, Litvinova suggests. 'Once he spoke about the despair he experienced after his father's death, when he found himself alone in a hostile world. Besides, he was incapable of resisting any form of force and boorishness. When pressure was exerted on him, he was ready to compromise himself, read out or sign anything, so long as he was left alone.' What followed was typical of his personality: anguish at what he was doing and the fawning from on high he received for it, scrupulous attention to his official duties, however trite or wretched; a shrug of resignation over the friends his decision had cost him. Before Lev Lebedinsky he wept. 'I'm scared to death of them. From childhood I've been doing things that I wanted not to do . . . I'm a wretched alcoholic . . . I've been a whore, I am and always will be a whore.'

Lebedinsky understood what he called 'the mask', and knew that the truth was in the music. In 1960 Shostakovich visited Dresden, where a Mosfilm unit was making a documentary about the rescue of art treasures. 'And this devastated city reminded me of our own devastated cities that I'd been in, and of the human victims, the many lives taken away by the war that Hitler's fascism unleashed. All this made such a profound impression on me that in three days I had a quartet completely finished.'

So much for the public rationale. A quotation from *Lady Macbeth* marks out the *Eighth Quartet* as a piece we might expect to be as secret and intensely individual as the *Eighth Symphony*. So it is: heart-rending music, as simple as plainchant, as eloquent as a denunciation, its opening as bare as a dirge. The DSCH motto and a quotation from the Song of Death identify its victims – the Jewish people, the composer himself; and the variations he works on two motifs create a consummate fusion of musical and human needs: the drama of brutalization, the tragedy and futility of tenderness among its ruins. A suppliant hand stretches out from Bomber Harris's rubble, and we forget the weightless mastery of counterpoint, of pace and theatre, that has made irony into a cry of anguish. The *Eighth Quartet* condenses the Symphony's agenda, makes it explicit; and it is capricious with a sense of awful possibility. It ends with the moan, 'Tormented by Grievous Bondage', which can also be translated, 'He Died a Slave.' Impossible to misinterpret, but Soviet critics did so; and they announced boisterously that 'in the finale, the composer quotes Lenin's favourite song'.

Inspirations rarely drop out of the blue, and the *Eighth* draws on vocabulary developed in its predecessor, which had been performed earlier in the year. The *Seventh* is a thirteen-minute, cyclic transmutation of material through despair to resignation. Its opening is a lone, almost furtive remembrance of Nina's intimacy and confidences: the *Lento* is a desolation as if leached by acid, through whose dust the need to make sense inches its way.

Lebedinsky asked why Shostakovich as a child had gone to the Finland Station in St Petersburg to see a famous homcoming. 'I wanted to hear Lenin's speech' was the reply. 'I knew a dictator was on his way.' But as a Party member, the prodigal son was compelled to write a Lenin symphony. This was in 1961, and the *Twelfth* was simply entitled '*1917*'. It was written at breakneck speed, but scarcely from conviction. The original plan had been to do a satire of Bolshevism, whose meaning would be clear to those who, said Shostakovich, 'had ears to hear.' Friends warned him it was too dangerous. Then Lebedinsky had a panic-stricken telephone call. 'I wrote the symphony' Shostakovich explained, 'and I realized you'd been right. They'd crucify me for it because my conception was an obvious caricature of Lenin. So I sat down and wrote another one in three or four days. And it's terrible!' With his insane technique, Lebedinsky adds, he could do anything. The television crews went away happy.

There was dynamite to come, on 18 December 1962. This was the occasion of the first performance of a *Thirteenth Symphony* for bass soloist, chorus and orchestra, to texts by the young poet Yevgeny Yevtuschenko – and a message so explosive that Shostakovich returned home to find KGB agents posted outside his apartment, in case he tried to defect.

Yevtushenko's poems had been published, to official disapproval. It was Shostakovich's distillation of their message that was devastating. *Babi Yar*, a denunciation of anti-Semitism in memory of the steep ravine where a race was put to death; *Humour*, a song in praise of non-conformity; *In the Store*, an expression of the suffering of millions of ordinary men and women in a police state; *Fears* ('Fears slithered everywhere, like shadows ... they taught us to keep silent when we should have screamed'). And then its finale, *A Career*, in honour of Galileo and Tolstoy, who had not been afraid to speak out: 'A certain scientist, Galileo's contemporary, was no more stupid than Galileo. He knew that the earth revolved, but he had a family.'

Krushchev demanded a ban. The square of Moscow's Conservatory Hall was sealed off by police cordons, the city buzzed with rumours, the singer fled. Mravinsky, such a monster in front of his orchestra, backed out in sheer panic. Boris Schwarz remembers the concert, conducted by Kirill Kondrashin:

> *The tension was unbearable. The first movement,* Babi Yar, *was greeted with a burst of spontaneous applause. At the end of the hour-long work, there was an ovation rarely witnessed. On the stage was Shostakovich, shy and awkward, bowing stiffly. He was joined by Yevtushenko, moving with the ease of a born actor. Two great artists – a generation apart – fighting for the same cause – freedom of the human spirit. Seeing the pair together, the audience went wild; the rhythmic clapping redoubled in intensity, the cadenced shouts 'Bra-vo Shos-ta-ko-vich!' and 'Bra-vo Yev-tu-shen-ko!' filled the air.*

*Babi Yar* is Shostakovich's choral masterpiece, held together by one compelling narrative voice. It brings a humanist's passion to the trudge of fear and hopelessness, the inertia of apathy, the throb of vacant calm between moments of horror, the rapturous tremor of possible salvation. Its swirling success lies in its juxtapositions of scale, for what it captures is as intimate as horror, as intimidating as the suffering of millions. It makes misery noble without ever losing its indignation that such things can be. Its prancing second movement, *Humour*, unearths Shostakovich's most defiant sarcasm in an attack from all angles, a dance as predatory as Salome's, spiked by brashly snapping percussion.

There squalling soprano winds (the little man, whining like Job) fight against the full torrent of an orchestra. The fourth movement, *Fears*, is a requiem for those unlucky enough still to be alive. Never have the dark wings of our slender mortality been made more palpable than in the sombre lustre of Shostakovich's orchestration: a black, guttural subsidence almost below the threshold of hearing, as if risen from catacombs. After all of that, *A Career* opens with a susurrus of birdsong – and at last the quiet voices of reason (embodied in counterpoint) and courage surmount everything. With a passing motif from *Humour*, now tinkling not on a bell but a glockenspiel, the symphony dies away in knowing forgiveness.

The *Thirteenth Symphony* was to be last of the wedding cakes in Cinemascope. His lean *Second Cello Concerto* of 1966 was dedicated to Rostropovich, as the *First* had been, and was performed on Shostakovich's sixtieth birthday. It begins with a soliloquy and ends in a joke, a deceptive false climax in which its scherzo theme returns as a cruel *memento mori*. Throughout this music an act of meditation is placed centre-stage, and the sense of nocturnal visitation is more profound than in 1959: the brooding artist and his audience are bound together through an organic cohesion that levitates in a space far removed from the limitations of orthodox concerto structure.

The sense of dialogue, of both reconciliation and adventure where once there could be only clamorous dialectic or browbeating, reflects Shostakovich's calm maturity. This is the secure face as an artist who knows that at last his untrammelled stream of thought will be made sense of and valued, who can be public in his loneliness. In the short space between cello concertos he has moved to the composure and synthesis of his final period – and no other composer could create an underworld of sound as compelling as he does here.

In any case, with unmistakable signs of the debilitating illness that was to finish Shostakovich off, with Krushchev deposed by Brezhnev's old guard, it was time for something new.

# CHAPTER 7
# ASSERTION, DEATH
## (1966–75)

- ♦ A new, lean idiom
- ♦ Shostakovich and Britten
- ♦ Honours and the contemplation of death
- ♦ The final masterworks

The fate of composers is either to re-invent themselves, or to atrophy. In 1963 Shostakovich had struck up a friendship with Benjamin Britten, and by 1966 the two composers' styles had begun to converge with a new energy, astringent and macabre. In Shostakovich's case too there had been a heart-attack, a presentiment of the shortness of life; and with it a hypnotic, a self-ironic study of life's constants: morality, time, love, betrayal, death. This is the language of the *Second Cello Concerto*, and of the *Eleventh Quartet* from the same year. The *Eleventh* opens with the quality of a fable, deliberately coy and bare. It is a typically wily move that a theme not for the violins but the cello – and one intimated almost incidentally – provides the material for its development. The *Eleventh* is one of Shostakovich's essays in an orthodoxy which is eaten away from the inside: setting out its case in circuitous phrases that slump back obsessively, falling as if to earth in a curiously Russian gesture of stoic helplessness. By the third movement, a *Recitative* marked by explosive dissonance, the process by which accepted meaning has been corroded, is complete. In the remainder of the piece, pent-up energy discharges like an overwound clock; and there is nothing fortuitous about the calculation, the sense of mechanization, with which Shostakovich reveals experience re-appraised in the hard light of day, worked and exhausted to the point of moral anaesthesia.

On his sixtieth birthday there seemed a desperate urge by

the Soviet authorities to make amends for what Shostakovich had suffered in the past. They smothered him with decorations – Hero of Socialist Labour, The Gold Hammer and Sickle, the Order of Lenin – while countries abroad outbid one other in honours and invitations. The composer himself was depressed. Journalists noted the wretchedly pallid stare and nervous, twitching fingers; 'the inscrutable face with its strange tremor' of a man prone to silent misery or a jabbering spate of words. His doctors had banned cigarettes and alcohol, and the result was a composer's block which it took smuggled brandy to cure. The outcome after three days' slog and a rare interlude of contentment, was the exquisite yet achingly depressive *Seven Romances on Poems of Alexander Blok*.

In September 1968 audiences heard his last optimistic finale, that of the *Twelfth Quartet*. He summons there the Beethovenian world of 'high ideals', in conflict with what he called 'the agonizing impossibility of solving the contradictions of life.' In the *Twelfth*, something of Schoenberg's serialist technique finds its way into a music that evolves with burnished symphonic breadth. 'Splendid', Shostakovich called it. Others heard 'the tread of death itself . . . the ultimate examination of the performers' interpretative powers.' It was Beethoven who remained Shostakovich's musical hero, and it is apt that each man's final and surmounting testimony is in the form of a quartet series. It has been said that chamber music threads through Shostakovich's creative life like some inner odyssey, and inhabits terrain of increasing spiritual desolation, as private and profound as Schubert's *Winterreise*. The last four quartets enter a world of human isolation, the contemplation of life's shortness, and scarified despair. Each was written for a different member of the Beethoven Quartet of Moscow, itself a national institution.

The *Thirteenth* was dedicated to the violist Vadim Borisovsky: a one-movement span, steeped in an awareness of mortality. It is, as Borisovsky's pupil Fyodor Druzhinin has observed, 'a hymn to the viola', with a stratospheric and resinous tessitura inspired by the tonal coloration the Beethovens brought to their performances of Bach. It is a forlorn association of ideas, rearing from a brooding Adagio to a grisly march and down again, in which fragments crystallize and overlap with immeasurable subtlety. The violist Alan George, who knew Shostakovich and his intentions, has compared it to a grey landscape upon which compulsion collapses into silence.

And well it might be. For Shostakovich was falling to bits, with what was tentatively diagnosed as a sort of poliomyelitis. From Garvriil Ilizarov's orthopaedic clinic in the Urals he announced the rewards of a strict regime: 'I can use my right hand to shave, do up my buttons. I don't miss my mouth with a spoon.' To Flora Litvinova he confided, 'I don't want to die yet. I still have a lot of music to write.' Another coronary meant an end to Ilizarov's exercises, and Shostakovich trained himself to write with his left hand, in case the right gave out. He watched with distaste as bones snapped.

The *Fourteenth Symphony* of 1969 is a confrontation with the prosaic ugliness of death – a drab and universal truth that lies as if in wait, the prospect it presents to those who foresee it. 'The devil take it,' said Shostakovich at rehearsals, carried away like a small boy in his excitement. 'I never knew it would sound so good.' He wanted a recording made instantly, convinced he was about to die. The idea of setting a cycle of poems on such a theme had come to him in 1962, when he had orchestrated Mussorgsky's *Songs and Dances of Death*. The gestation, then, was longer than that of the *Tenth Symphony*; and it shows in the *Fourteenth's* enormity of thought and tight concentration, its chilling restraint and beauty, in which the only humour is one bitter laugh, and comfort is as ephemeral as mist. There are newer acknowledgments too: not least of the creative rapport with Britten, as Shostakovich speaks of the immortality of art and friendship.

This is the redemption to which Shostakovich returns in the *Suite on the Poems of Michelangelo*, which he set five years later:

> *Here fate has sent me eternal sleep*
> *But I am not dead.*
> *Though buried in the earth*
> *I live in you,*
> *Whose lamentations I listen to,*
> *Since friend is reflected in friend . . .*
> *That means I am not dust*
> *And mortal decay does not touch me.*

The use of percussion in these last symphonies establishes them as a trilogy. He chooses a bell sound, as Mahler had in *The Song of the Earth*, to establish a prescient gloom and fatalism. The death of Lorelei in the *Fourteeth*, the tolling of *Babi Yar*, the eerie tinkles of the *Fifteenth* – all of them engender immense effect through minimal resources. This is because percussion instruments are both illustrative and laconic. Each time 'the blonde witch' Lorelei thinks of death, we hear her agitation in the crack of xylophones and a temple block. As Tatyana Kazakova explains, 'She cannot cope with her catastrophic thought of committing suicide, but at the same time her future is predestined: Lorelei is doomed to die. Increasingly the persistent beats reflect her growing determination.' The culmination of this movement is no less than a savage lashing of sound.

The purpose of the *Fourteenth Symphony*, then, is to appraise the razed anatomy of human fate, the dissolution of enfeebled flesh. Its basis has affinities with the sardonic language of Stravinsky's *Soldier's Tale*, enlarged so as to encompass the imagery of sacrifice and betrayal, fatal infatuation, incestuous love, suicide ('three tall lilies powdered with gold that the wind scares'). Above them all stands the tyrannous omnipotence and overwhelming presence of death: the depths and landscapes of a dying face 'like a fruit rotting in the air.' Shostakovich's conclusion quotes Rilke:

> *Death is great,*
> *we belong to it*
> *with its laughing mouth.*
> *When we think we are in the midst of life*
> *death dares to weep*
> *within us.*

This is something tart and eerie – dark, rank, voluptuous – but charged too with the overwrought vibrancy of Benjamin Britten, so that in *Malaguena* and *Lorelei* the music, unable to contain itself, bursts out on a dizzy career of its own. 'The smell of salt and blood,' as Lorca said, is what Shostakovich contemplates. He dissects circumstances as sharply as a surgeon, his pity as relentlessly unsentimental as an etching by Egon Schiele, as sorry and as arid as a bell heard through air scorched with dust. The furtive interlude of *In the Santé* is as near to silence as music can be:

*In a pit like a bear*
*Each morning I walk*
*Let's go around and around for ever*
*The sky is blue like a chain . . .*

*The noise of my chained chair*
*Have pity on my tearless eyes, on my pallor . . .*
*Have pity above all on my faltering mind*
*And this despair overcoming it.*

The *Fourteenth* was dedicated to Britten, who conducted the western premiere, picking up the score after its performance to kiss it. Roy Blokker rightly concludes, 'It forms a bridge between life and death, between total abandon and the often inaccessible philosophical confrontation with the spectre of dying. If Shostakovich is to be remembered for only one work, this symphony may well be that work.'

There is an afterword concerning the first Moscow performance. Shostakovich had spoken to his audience about the need to die with a clear conscience, 'so that one need not be ashamed of oneself.' In the fifth movement there was a commotion as a man leapt up and fled. It was the last of his old Stalinist tormentors, Pavel Apostolov, who was found lifeless outside the building from a heart-attack.

The last quartets share a funeral-march rhythm. The *Fourteenth* intermingles innocence and experience, the childlike and sophisticated, in measures of tenderness, nostalgia, humour and inscrutability: a private farewell as life and its riches slip away. The composer Alfred Schnittke has drawn attention to the links between this quartet and Shostakovich's final symphony, which were completed twenty-two months apart. 'They are the most original landmarks in time, where the past enters into new relations with the present, invades musical reality – like the ghost of Hamlet's father – and reshapes it.'

The *Fifteenth Symphony* had its first performance in January 1972. As Maxim Shostakovich has affirmed, it has connections not only with the pantomime of the *Ninth Symphony*, but most of all – in its instrumentation and structure – the *Fourth*.

Casting our minds back to 1936 shows us how far Shostakovich has come. For both are works impelled by the threat not only of dehumanization, but of chaos. In the final symphony the apocalyptic flamboyance of the *Fourth* has been supplanted by subtler wit and terse, almost sinister, composure. The *Fourth* mapped exuberantly the horizon of a young composer who saw the Pacific stretch out before him, as Cortez had done. It was a balletic exhibition for a stage that could never be; whereas the final symphony is the introspection of a man whose vital sinews might at any moment break, who has learnt to balance his mastery on a spider's web: who proceeds in his meditations with the deliberate stealth of a spider, knowing that he is eavesdropped upon by the world. And what a weight of craftsmanship he has gained: a frigid compactness of texture and timing, its heroics withered into pathos to bear a structure that is at once sly, obstinate and refractory.

Yet the emotional tenor of these two symphonies is the same. They share an interplay of emotionalism and alienation, automatism and a quixotic sense of discovery, playfulness and deadly irony. In the *Fifteenth* both the control and the dispossession are more complete: for if the *Fourth* was driven by the foreboding of some dreadful inevitability that must end beyond despair, the *Fifteenth* is emotionally indeterminate. Harmonic and tonal incongruity play their part in that, and both help to create the impression of expanded and far-flung space beneath which morose and disparate elements intrude upon some state of absolute musical impaction. Yet the principal undermining mechanism is the rigidity of tempo. Each movement seems trapped in its own temporal frame – whether flippancy so dogged that it verges on the tragic, or the ritual trudge of a wake – and throughout, there is an allusive and calculated obliqueness of gesture. If the *Fourth* clamoured for attention, the *Fifteenth* not once looks us in the eye. The sense of disorientation is as complete, and as infallible, as the logic.

Mention of logic is appropriate here, for if each of Shostakovich's symphonic trilogies ends with a return to well-balanced classical writing and apparent good humour, his last is no exception. Yet if the *Fifteenth* is simply about a cloudless sky, as Shostakovich claimed in his Collected Edition, what are we to make of its references to the funeral music in Wagner's *Siegfried*, the Fate motif of *The Ring*, the Prelude to *Tristan und Isolde*, the quotations from the *Leningrad Symphony*? It would be more true to say that Shostakovich adopts the mantle of Kovrin in Chekhov's *The Black*

*Monk*, a member of God's elect who reveals truths to his be-nighted fellows in an age stripped of heroes. Again, Maxim has confirmed the views of Soviet musicologists, that his father's symphony is about the cyclic nature of human life – from a child's naivety to the sober gaze of one who has learned to accept a realism that at least allows us to create our own moments of beauty.

Yet it had always been the shock of newly-discovered pain that kept Dmitri going. His final quartet of 1974 is great, coura-geous music: sparse in its gestures, and in texture as dry as a bone. Shostakovich has been called a Schubert for our times, and the spiritual affinities are nowhere clearer than here. The *Fifteenth Quartet* is an arch-structure of six unbroken movements, as if summoned from extinction before ever they came to be; and unfolding at the tempo of some nocturnal march into a morose psychological conflict that relapses into spectral trills. It is music informed, made uncanny, by an awareness of existence passing into the infinity of oblivion. It is an act of progressive self-trans-figuration, the considered innocence of a second and higher artistic childhood: for it contains the clarity and vulnerability of pristine perception, the burden of disillusionment. We are con-fronted, seemingly, with the phosphorescent trace of some secret illusion to which the composer has uncompromised fidelity: a sparse melodic line above which harmonies elide and evaporate like mist. Within its span a life's influences (Mahlerian *Ländler*, polyphony and the cavernous modalities of church music: the dislocations, the rhythmic treadmills and sporadic eruptions of drama, which a lifetime's mastery of musical stagecraft and tim-ing allow) are drawn into a seamless and private conception whose organic tensions lie beyond irony, beyond any guile at all. In its self-preoccupation it is both masterful and oddly helpless. One recognizes that, to the end of his life, Shostakovich was just as much a disappointed innocent as Schubert had been.

You could tell when another heart-attack was creeping up, he said, because you got no pleasure from vodka. Shostakovich succumbed to the last of them, in Moscow, on 9 August 1975.

Five days later, as windy speeches rolled over a tarted-up corpse and a military band butchered its way through the Chopin *Funeral March*, the lid of his coffin was hammered down at the Novodevichi Cemetery. A professor from the Central Music

School muttered, 'This is the end of the road. Full stop.' It began to drizzle.

In the *Fourteenth Symphony* Shostakovich quotes Küchelbecker. 'What consolation is there in talent amidst rogues and fools?' Yet from Apollinaire he has already found his answer:

> *Daylight disappears and now a lamp*
> *Burns in the prison.*
> *We are alone in my cell*
> *Lovely brightness, Beloved reason*

The Soviet composer, Sofiya Gubaidulina, remembered her old teacher with infinite gratitude. 'He sensed my pain. Shostakovich's sensitivity to a musical phenomenon that lay outside his own sphere stemmed from his own vulnerability. . . . Despite his outward irony, his manner of expressing himself in paradoxes, he felt and understood the suffering that Russians are doomed to endure, and the manner in which it defines their behaviour and their relationships. His influence was all-important to us, and it formulated our attitude to life. He was the person from whom young people hoped to receive the answers.'

Alfred Schnittke, spiritual heir to this music, appraised it best in the year of his mentor's death. 'It is now fifty years that music has been under the influence of Shostakovich. In the twentieth century only Stravinsky was endowed with this same magic ability to subordinate everything coming into his field of vision for himself. . . . When in Shostakovich the images of his own musical past meet up in collages with images from the history of music an astonishing effect of objectification occurs, of introducing the individual to the universal; and it is in this way that the greatest challenge in the life of the artist is solved: to influence the world through confluence with the world.'

'When man is happy,' declared a Soviet film-maker, 'eternal themes rarely interest him.' One of the functions of writing, certainly, is to make new our sense of loss: to regain, as Anna Akhmatova put it, 'a gift we've lost – to weep.' At the end of his reminiscences – and of his life – Shostakovich confessed:

> *There were no particularly happy moments in my life, no great*
> *joys. It was drab and dull and it makes me sad to think about*

it. Man feels joy when he's healthy and happy. I was often ill.
I'm ill now, and my illness deprives me of the opportunity to
take pleasure in ordinary things. It's hard for me to walk. I'm
teaching myself to write with my left hand in case my right one
gives out completely. I am utterly in the hands of the doctors,
and I take all the medicine they prescribe, even if it sickens me.
Now all they talk about is courage.

But I don't feel like a superman yet, super-courageous. I'm
a weak man, and no treatment seems to help. . . . When I'm in
Moscow, I feel worst of all. I keep thinking that I'll fall and
break a leg. I'm afraid to go out. I'm terrified of being seen, I
feel so fragile, breakable.

No, every new day of my life brings me no joy. I thought
I would find distraction reminiscing about my old friends
and acquaintances. Some of these people played an important
role in my life, and I felt it was my duty to tell what I still
remembered about them. Yet even this undertaking has turned
out to be a sad one. I thought my life was replete with sorrow,
that it would be hard to find a more miserable man. But
when I started going over the stories of my friends and
acquaintances, I was horrified. Not one of them had an easy
or a happy life. Some came to a dreadful end, some died in
suffering, and the life of many of them could easily be described
as more miserable than mine.

That made me even sadder. I was remembering my friends,
and all I saw was corpses, mountains of corpses. And the picture
filled me with horrible depression. I'm sad, I'm grieving all the
time. . . .

I went on. I forced myself and went on remembering . . . I
reasoned this way: I've seen many unpleasant and tragic events,
as well as several sinister and repulsive figures. My relations
with them brought me much sorrow and suffering. And I
thought, perhaps my experience could be of some use to people
younger than I? Perhaps they wouldn't have the terrible disillusionment that I had to face, and perhaps they would go
through life better prepared, more hardened, than I was. Perhaps their lives would be free from the bitterness that has
coloured my life grey.

Andrei Tarkovsky was to say in *Solaris* that shame is the feeling that saves mankind. This is Shostakovich's legacy for our century, and for any era in which people are degraded and robbed of their humanity. He is our compassion, our need to fight on against hopeless adversity, our irrepressible and courageous humour – but best of all, he is our sense of shame.

# SELECTED
# FURTHER READING

The revolution that has taken place over recent years in our understanding of Shostakovich, following *Testimony*, has created a demand for answers that a handful of books have successfully addressed. Doubts over the veracity of *Testimony* itself were quick to emerge, despite later evidence that it seems true to at least the spirit of Shostakovich: it is, perhaps, the strip-cartoon portrait of his life. Ian MacDonald's biography was an attempt to make sense of this debate by returning to the evidence of music. It is still commendable, despite charges that it inferred too much from limited analysis.

Eric Roseberry's study, inclined to underplay the bitterness of Shostakovich's era as well as his private struggle, is a good illustrated introduction to the times.

The best appraisal of 'Shostakovich the man' that we are ever likely to have is Elizabeth Wilson's magnificent *A Life Remembered*, simply because it gathers the accounts of scores of the people who knew him.

## FIRST PORTS OF CALL:

Roy Blokker with Robert Dearling: *The Music of Dmitri Shostakovich – The Symphonies* (Associated University Presses, 1979)

Robert Conquest: *The Great Terror* (Hutchinson, 1990)

Edited by David Fanning: *Shostakovich Studies* (Cambridge University Press, 1995)

Ian MacDonald: *The New Shostakovich* (Oxford University Press, 1991)

Edited by Christopher Norris: *Shostakovich: The man and his Music* (Lawrence and Wishart, 1982)

Robert Ottaway: *Shostakovich Symphonies* (BBC Music Guides, 1978)

Eric Roseberry: *Shostakovich* (Omnibus Press, 1981, 1986)

As related to Solomon Volkov: *Testimony: The memoirs of Dmitri Shostakovich* (Hamish Hamilton, 1979)

Elizabeth Wilson: *Shostakovich: A Life Remembered* (Faber and Faber, 1994)

## FOR THOSE WHO TAKE THEIR SHOSTAKOVICH VERY SERIOUSLY:

David Fanning: *The Breadth of the Symphonist* (Royal Musical Association, London, 1988)

Richard M Longman: *Expression and Structure: Processes of Integration in the Large-Scale Instrumental Music of Dmitri Shostakovich* (Garland Publishing, Inc., New York, 1989)

Tatyana Kazakova: *Orchestral Style Development in the Symphonies of Dmitri Shostakovich* (MA dissertation, California State University, 1983)

Eric Roseberry: *Ideology, Style, Content, and Thematic Process in the Symphonies, Cello Concertos and String Quartets of Shostakovich* (Garland Publishing Inc., New York, 1989)

# DMITRI SHOSTAKOVICH: COMPLETE LIST OF WORKS

*Scherzo in F sharp minor for Orchestra*, Opus 1 (1919)

*Eight Preludes for Piano*, Opus 2 (1919–20)

*Five Preludes for Piano* (1920–21)

*Theme with Variations in B minor* for Orchestra, Opus 3 (1921–22)

*Two Fables of Krilov* (for mezzo-soprano and orchestra) Opus 4 (1922)

Three *Fantastic Dances* for Piano, Opus 5 (1922)

*Suite in F sharp minor* for Two Pianos, Opus 6 (1922)

*Scherzo in E flat* for Orchestra, Opus 7 (1924)

*Trio No.1*, Opus 8 (1923)

Three *Pieces for Cello and Piano*, Opus 9 (1923–24, lost)

*Symphony No.1 in F minor*, Opus 10 (1924–25)

*Two Pieces* (Prelude and Scherzo) *for String Octet*, Opus 11 (1924–25)

*Sonata No.1 for Piano*, Opus 12 (1926)

*Aphorisms for Piano*, Opus 13 (1927)

*Symphony No.2 in B* for Orchestra and Chorus, '*October*': Opus 14 (1927)

*The Nose* (opera in three acts), Opus 15 (1927–28)

*Suite* from *The Nose*, Opus 15a (1927–28)

*Tahiti Trot* ('*Tea for Two*', arranged for orchestra), Opus 16 (1928)

Two *Scarlatti Pieces* (transcription for wind orchestra) Opus 17 (1928)

Film music: *New Babylon* Opus 18 (1928)

*The Bedbug* (incidental music to Mayakovsky's play), Opus 19 (1919)

*Symphony No.3 in E flat* for Orchestra with Chorus, '*The First of May*': Opus 20 (1929)

*Six Romances on words by Japanese Poets* (for tenor and orchestra) Opus 21 (1928–32)

*The Age of Gold* (ballet in three acts), Opus 22 (1927–30)

*Suite* from *The Age of Gold* for Orchestra, Opus 22a (1929–32)

Polka from *The Age of Gold* for Piano (1935, duet version 1962)

*Two Pieces* for an Opera *Columbus*, Opus 23 (1929, lost)

*The Gunshot* (incidental music to Bezymensky's play), Opus 24 (1929, lost)

*Virgin Soil* (incidental music to Gorbenko and Lyov's play), Opus 25 (1929, lost)

Film-music: *Alone*, Opus 26 (1930–31)

*The Bolt* (choreographic spectacle in three acts), Opus 27 (1930–31)

*Suite* for Orchestra from *The Bolt* (Ballet Suite No.5), Opus 27a (1931)

*Rule Britannia!* (incidental music to Pyotrovsky's play), Opus 28 (1931)

Opera: *Lady Macbeth of the Mtsensk District*, Opus 29 (1930–32)

Film-music: *Golden Mountains*, Opus 30 (1931, lost)

*Suite* for Orchestra from *Golden Mountains*, Opus 30a (1931)

*Conditional Death* (music for a music-hall review), Opus 31 (1931)

*Hamlet* (music for Shakespeare's tragedy), Opus 32 (1931–32)

*Hamlet*: (Suite for Small Orchestra from the Theatre Music), Opus 32a (1932)

*From Karl Marx to our own Days* (Symphonic Poem for Orchestra and Chorus) (1932)

Film-music: *Encounter*, Opus 33 (1932)

'*We meet this Morning*' (song for voice and piano from *Encounter*: 1932)

Twenty-four *Preludes for Piano*, Opus 34 (1932–33)

*Concerto No.1 in C minor* for Piano, Strings and Trumpet: Opus 35 (1933)

Music for a cartoon-film: *The Tale of the Priest and his worker Balda*, Opus 36 (1936)

*The Human Comedy* (incidental music to Balzac's play), Opus 37 (1933–34)

*Suite* No.1 for Jazz Orchestra (1934)

Film-music: *Love and Hate*, Opus 38 (1934)

*Bright Stream* (comedy-ballet in three acts), Opus 39 (1934–35)

*Sonata in D minor* for Cello and Piano, Opus 40 (1934)
Film-music: *Maxim's Youth* (*The Bolshevik*), Opus 41 (i) (1934–35)
Film-music: *Girl Companions*, Opus 41 (ii) (1934–35)
*Five Fragments* for Small Orchestra, Opus 42 (1935)
*Symphony No.4 in C minor*, Opus 43 (1935–36)
*Salute to Spain* (incidental music to Afinogenov's play), Opus 44 (1936)
Film-music: *Maxim's Return*, Opus 45 (1936–37)
*Four Romances on verses of Pushkin* (for bass and piano), Opus 46 (1936)
*Symphony No.5 in D minor*, Opus 47 (1937)
Film-music: *Volochayevska Days*, Opus 48 (1936–37)
*String Quartet No.1 in C*, Opus 49 (1938)
*Suite No.2* for Jazz Orchestra (1938)
Film-music: *Vybvorg District*, Opus 50 (1938)
Fragments from the *Maxim* film-trilogy, Opus 50a (assembled from Opp.41i), 45 & 50) (1938)
Film-music: *Friends*, Opus 51 (1938)
Film-music: *The Great Citizen* (Part 1), Opus 52 (1938)
Film-music: *Man at Arms* (also called *November*), Opus 53 (1938)
*Symphony No.6 in B minor*, Opus 54 (1939)
Film-music: *The Great Citizen* (Part 2), Opus 55 (1939)
Music for a cartoon film: *Stupid Little Mouse*, Opus 56 (1939, lost)
*Piano Quintet in G minor*, Opus 57 (1940)
*Boris Godunov* (re-orchestration of Mussorgsky's opera), Opus 58 (1939–40)
*Three Pieces* for Violin (originally Opus 59; apparently withdrawn: 1940)
*King Lear* (incidental music to Shakespeare's tragedy), Opus 58a (1940)
Film-music: *Korzinka's Adventure*, Opus 59 (1940, lost)
*Symphony No.7 in C*, '*Leningrad* ', Opus 60 (1941)
*Sonata No.2 in B minor* for Piano, Opus 61 (1942)
*Six Romances on verses of English Poets* (for bass and piano), Opus 62 (1942)
*Suite* for theatre-show: *Native Leningrad*, Opus 63 (1942)
*The Gamblers* (unfinished opera after Gogol, originally Opus 63: 1941)

*The Vow of the People's Commissar* (song for Bass, Chorus and Orchestra: 1942)

*Symphony No.8 in C minor*, Opus 65 (1943)

Film-music: *Zoya*, Opus 64 (1944)

*Suite* for dancing: *Russian River*, Opus 66 (1944)

*Eight English and American Folksongs* (for low voice and orchestra: 1944)

*Piano Trio No.2 in E minor*, Opus 67 (1944)

*String Quartet No.2 in A*, Opus 68 (1944)

*Children's Notebook: Six Pieces for Piano*, Opus 69 (1944–45)

*Symphony No.9 in E flat*, Opus 70 (1945)

Film-music: *Simple Folk*, Opus 71 (1945)

*Two Songs* for Voice and Piano, Opus 72 (1945)

*String Quartet No.3 in F*, Opus 73 (1946)

Cantata: '*Poem of the Motherland* ', Opus 74 (1947)

Film-music: *Young Guards*, Opus 75 (1947–48)

*Suite* from the music to *Young Guards*, Opus 75a (1948)

Film-music: *Pirogov*, Opus 76 (1947)

*Suite* from the music to *Pirogov*, Opus 76a (1947)

*Violin Concerto No.1 in A minor*, Opus 77 (1947–48)

Film-music: *Michurin*, Opus 78 (1948)

*Suite* from the music to *Michurin*, Opus 78a (1948)

Film-music: *Meeting on the Elbe*, Opus 80 (1948)

'*Homesickness*' (from *Meeting on the Elbe*) for Voice and Piano (1956)

*Suite* from the music to *Meeting on the Elbe*, Opus 80a (?1948)

*From Jewish Folk-Poetry* (cycle for soprano, contralto and tenor with piano), Opus 79 (1948)

*The Song of the Forests* (oratorio), Opus 81 (1949)

Chorus: '*In the Fields stand the Collective Farms*' (from *The Song of the Forests*, arranged probably in 1960)

'*A Walk into the Future*' (song from *The Song of the Forests*, arranged probably in 1962)

Film-music: *The Fall of Berlin*, Opus 82 (1949)

Song: '*Beautiful Day*' (from *The Fall of Berlin*, arranged in 1950)

*Suite* from *The Fall of Berlin*, 82a (assembled 1950)

*Ballet Suite No.1*, for Orchestra (1949)

*String Quartet No.4 in D*, Opus 83 (1949)

*Two Romances on verses by Mikhail Lermontov*, for male voice and piano, Opus 84 (1950)

Film-music: *Byelinsky*, Opus 85 (1950)
*Suite* for Chorus and Orchestra from *Byelinsky*, Opus 85a (1950)
*Four Songs* to Words by Dolmatovsky, Opus 86 (1951)
*Twenty-four Preludes and Fugues* for Piano, Opus 87 (1950–51)
*Ten Poems on texts by Revolutionary Poets* (for soloists and chorus a cappella), Opus 88 (1951)
*Ballet Suite No.2*, for Orchestra (1951)
Film-music: *The Memorable Year 1919*, Opus 89 (1951)
Fragments for Orchestra from the Music to *The Memorable Year 1919*, Opus 89a (1951)
Cantata: '*The Sun shines over our Motherland* ', Opus 90 (1952)
*Four Monologues on verses of Pushkin*, for bass and piano: Opus 91 (1952)
*Ballet Suite No.3*, for Orchestra (1952)
*String Quartet No.5 in B flat*, Opus 92 (1952)
*Ballet Suite No.4*, for Orchestra (1953)
*Symphony No.10 in E minor*, Opus 93 (1953)
*Concertino* for two pianos, Opus 94 (1953)
Film-music: *Song of a Great River*, Opus 95 (1954)
*Festival Overture*, Opus 96 (1954)
Film-music: *The Gadfly*, Opus 97 (1955)
Tarantella from *The Gadfly*, for two pianos (1963)
*Fragments for Orchestra* from the music for *The Gadfly*, Opus 97a (1955)
*Five Romances* (*Songs of Our Days*) for bass and piano, Opus 98 (1954)
Film-music: *The First Echelon*, Opus 99 (1956)
*Fragments for Chorus and Orchestra* from *The First Echelon*, Opus 99a (1956)
*Six Spanish Songs* for Soprano and Orchestra, Opus 100 (1956)
*String Quartet No.6 in G*, Opus 101 (1956)
*Piano Concerto No.2 in F*, Opus 102 (1957)
*Symphony No.11 in G minor*, '*The Year 1905* ', Opus 103 (1957)
*Two Russian Folksong Adaptations*, for Soloists and a cappella Chorus, Opus 104 (1957)
Musical comedy: *Moscow, Cheremushki*, Opus 105 (1956)
*Khovanschina* (orchestration of Mussorgsky's opera), Opus 106 (1959)
*Cello Concerto No.1 in E flat*, Opus 107 (1959)

*String Quartet No.7 in F sharp minor*, Opus 108 (1960)

*Satires* (*Pictures of the Past*: five romances for soprano and piano),
    Opus 109 (1960)

*String Quartet No.8 in C minor*, Opus 110 (1960)

*Novorossiysk Chimes* (*The Fire of Eternal Glory*) for orchestra
    (1960)

Film-music: *Five Days – Five Nights*, Opus 111 (1960)

*Suite* from the music for *Five Days – Five Nights*, Opus 111a
    (1960)

*Symphony No.12 in D minor*, '*1917*', Opus 112 (1961)

*Dances of the Dolls*: Suite for Piano (1952–62)

Film-music: *Cheremushki* (based on the musical show) (1962)

*Songs and Dances of Death* (orchestration of Mussorgsky) (1962)

*Symphony No.13 in B flat*: *Babi Yar*, Opus 113 (1962)

*Katerina Ismailova* (revision of opera, Opus 29), Opus 114
    (1956)

*Suite* in Five Scenes for Orchestra, from *Katerina Ismailova*
    (1956)

*From Jewish Folk-Poetry* (orchestration of Opus 79) (1963)

*Overture on Russian and Kirghiz Folk Themes*, Opus 115 (1963)

Film-music: *Hamlet*, Opus 116 (1963–64)

*Suite* for Orchestra from the music to *Hamlet*, Opus 116a (1964)

*String Quartet No.9 in E flat*, Opus 117 (1964)

*String Quartet No.10 in A flat*, Opus 118 (1964)

*Cantata* for Bass, Chorus and Orchestra: '*The Execution of Stepan
    Rapin*', Opus 119 (1964)

Film-music: *A Year in the Life*, Opus 120 (1965)

*Five Romances* on texts from *Krokodil* magazine (for bass and
    piano), Opus 121 (1965)

*String Quartet No.11 in F minor*, Opus 122 (1966)

*Preface to the Complete Collection of my Works, and Brief Reflections
    apropos this Preface* (for bass and piano), Opus 123 (1966)

*Two Choruses after Davidenko*, Opus 124 (1962)

*Cello Concerto in A minor* (by Schumann: re-orchestrated by
    Shostakovich for Rostropovich), Opus 125 (1963)

*Cello Concerto No.2 in G*, Opus 126 (1966)

*Seven Romances for Soprano and Piano Trio on Poems of Alexander
    Blok*, Opus 127 (1967)

*Spring, Spring* (for bass and piano: Opus 129) (1967)

*Funeral-Triumphant Prelude* for Orchestra, Opus 130 (1967)

*Symphonic Poem* for Orchestra: '*October*', Opus 131 (1967)

Film-music: *Sofya Perovoskaya*, Opus 132 (1967)

*String Quartet No.12 in D flat*, Opus 133 (1968)

*Sonata for Violin and Piano*, Opus 134 (1968)

*Symphony No.14* for Bass, Strings and Percussion, Opus 135 (1969)

*Eight Ballads* for Male Chorus: '*Loyalty*', Opus 136 (1970)

Film-music: *King Lear*, Opus 137 (1970)

*String Quartet No.13 in B flat minor*, Opus 138 (1970)

*March of the Soviet Militia* (for wind orchestra, Opus 139) (1970)

*Six Romances on Verses of English Poets* (orchestration of Opus 62), Opus 140 (1971)

*Symphony No.15 in A*, Opus 141 (also as arrangement for two pianos) (1971)

*String Quartet No.14 in F sharp minor*, Opus 142 (1972)

*Suite* for Contralto and Piano: *Six poems of Marina Tsvetaeva*, Opus 143 (1973)

*Six poems of Marina Tsvetaeva* (version for contralto and small orchestra), Opus 143a (1973)

*String Quartet No.15 in E flat minor*, Opus 144 (1974)

*Suite* for Bass and Piano on Verses of Michelangelo Buonarroti, Opus 145 (1974)

*Suite* on Verses of Michelangelo Buonarroti (version for bass and orchestra), Opus 145a (1974)

*Four Verses of Capitan Lebjadkin* (for bass and piano) Opus 146 (1974)

*Sonata* for Viola and Piano, Opus 147 (1975)

Ballet in Four Acts: *The Dreamers* (1975) (Largely drawn from the music of *The Bolt* and *The Age of Gold*, with some new material.)

*Symphony No.16*(?) [Reports were circulating in the West shortly before Shostakovich's death that he had completed two movements of a Sixteenth Symphony. But the Russian authorities have yet to confirm the existence of this work.]

# DMITRI SHOSTAKOVICH: RECOMMENDED RECORDINGS

**W**orks are listed first, followed by details of the artists and the disc number. All serial numbers apply to compact disc but some recordings can also be bought on tape cassette.

Shostakovich, like other twentieth-century composers, has been a particular victim of the recession said to be sweeping the record industry: and the dated analogue recordings of his great Soviet interpreters have been hit worst of all. Where there are doubts over whether a disc is still available, or whether some listeners might tolerate its technical roughness, a digital alternative has been given where this of sufficient merit to offer real choice. The dispiriting thing about preparing this list has been to witness how, as our command of sound technology advances, so an insight into interpretations that the composer himself might recognize and endorse is beginning to recede into the past. Not always – but all too often.

The good news is that BMG has gained the rights to the Melodiya archive, including those performances currently being withdrawn by Olympia and Praga. Already a remastering of Kirill Kondrashin's authentic set of symphonies is promised for 1997, and one hopes that other treasures will find their way back to the prominence they deserve.

A list of the abbreviations used here appears at the end of this section.

## CHAMBER AND INSTRUMENTAL MUSIC

**Twenty-Four Preludes for Piano, Opus 34** (with **Three Fantastic Dances** and **Piano Sonata No.2**)
- ♦  Nikolayeva (⊗ Hyperion CDA 66620)
- ♦  Also commended (with Alkan *Opus 31 Préludes*): Mustonen (⊗ Decca 433 055-2DH)

### Twenty Four Preludes and Fugues for Piano, Opus 87
- Nikolayeva (⊗ BMG / Melodiya 74321198492: 3 CDs)
- Also recommended: Nikolayeva (⊗ Hyperion CDA66441 / 3: 3 CDs)

### Quartet No.8 in C minor, Opus 110 (with Quartets Nos.6 & 9)
- The Shostakovich Quartet (⊗ Olympia OCD 533)

### Quartet No.15 in E flat minor, Opus 144
- (with *Quartets Nos.10 & 11*) The Shostakovich Quartet (⊗ Olympia OCD 534)
- (with *Quartets Nos.7 & 8*) The Beethoven Quartet (⊗ Consonance 81-3006)

## Also recommended:

### Quartets Nos.1, 2, 4
- The Shostakovich Quartet (⊗ Olympia OCD 531)

### Quartets Nos.1, 3, 4
- Tanejev Quartet (⊗ Leningrad Masters LM 1325)

### Quartets Nos.2, 5, 7
- The Shostakovich Quartet (⊗ Olympia OCD 532)

### Quartets Nos.12, 13, 14
- The Shostakovich Quartet (⊗ Olympia OCD 535)

### Quartets Nos.4, 8 & 11
- The Coull Quartet (⊗ ASV CD DCA 631 – digital recording)

### Quartets Nos.9, 10 & 11
- The Beethoven Quartet (⊗ Consonance 881-3009)

### Quartets Nos.3, 7 & 8
- The Borodin Quartet (⊗ Virgin 0777 7590412-3 – digital recording)

### String Quartets 1–15 (complete – 6 CDs)
♦ Fitzwilliam Quartet (⊗ Decca Enterprise 433 078-2DM6)

### Two Pieces for String Octet, Opus 11
♦ ASMF Chamber Ensemble (with Enescu, Richard Strauss) (⊗ Chandos CHAN 9131)

### Sonata for Cello and Piano in D minor, Opus 40
♦ Turovsky (vlc), Edlina (pf) (with Prokofiev: *Sonata*) (⊗ Chandos CHAN 8340)

### Piano Quintet in G minor, Opus 57
♦ Prime recommendation (deleted, with *Quartets Nos.7 & 8*): Richter (pf), Borodin Quartet (⊗ EMI CDC7 47507-2)
♦ Available commendation (with *Piano Trio No.2 in E minor*, Opus 67): Beaux Arts Trio: Drucker (vln), Dutton (vla) (⊗ Philips 432 079-2PH)

### Sonata for Violin and Piano, Opus 134
♦ Mordkovitch (vln), Benson (pf) (with Prokofiev, Schnittke) (⊗ Chandos CHAN 8988)

### Sonata for Viola and Piano, Opus 147
♦ (with Britten: *Lachrymae* and Stravinsky: *Elégie*, 1944) Zimmermann (vla): Höll (pf) (⊗ EMI CDC 754394-2)

## SYMPHONIC AND ORCHESTRAL WORKS

### Symphonies 1–15
♦ Moscow PO: Kondrashin (⊗ BMG / Melodiya 74321199522: 10-CD set, oas)

### Symphony No.1 in F minor, Opus 10 (with Symphony No.6)
♦ SNO: Järvi (⊗ Chandos CHAN 8411)

### Symphonies No.2 in B, Opus 14 ('To October'): No.3 in E flat, Opus 20 ('The First of May')
♦ London SO: Rostropovich (⊗ Teldec 4509-90853-2)

### Symphony No.4 in C minor, Opus 43
♦ Moscow PO: Kondrashin (⊗ BMG / Melodiya 74321198402)
♦ Digital recommendation SNO: Järvi (⊗ Chandos CHAN 8640)

### Symphony No.5 in D minor, Opus 47
♦ Mravinsky, Leningrad PO. Various recordings: (alone, at medium price) ⊗ Erato 2292-45752-2; (with Kosler's interpretation of *Symphony No.9*) ⊗ Praga PR 250 085 (if available); (bargain price, and a recent recording) ⊗ Leningrad Masters LM 1311; (with Salamonov's *Symphony No.2*) ⊗ Russian Disc RD CD 11 023
♦ Digital recommendation: SNO: Järvi (⊗ Chandos CHAN 8650) (with *Ballet Suite No.5* from *The Bolt*)

### Symphony No.6 in B minor, Opus 54
♦ SNO: Järvi (⊗ Chandos CHAN 8411) (with *Symphony No.1*)
♦ Also commended: Concertgebouw: Haitink (⊗ Decca 425 067-2DM) (with *Symphony No.12*)

### Symphony No.7 in C, Opus 60: 'Leningrad'
♦ SNO: Järvi (⊗ Chandos CHAN 8623)

### Symphony No.8 in C minor, Opus 65
♦ Leningrad PO: Mravinsky (⊗ Philips 422 442-2PH)
♦ Leningrad PO: Mravinsky (⊗ Russian Disc RD CD 10 917)
♦ Digital recommendation: SNO: Järvi (⊗ Chandos CHAN 8757)

### Symphony No.10 in E minor, Opus 93
♦ BPO: Karajan (⊗ DG 439 036-2)
♦ Also commended: SNO, Järvi – with *Ballet Suite No.4* (⊗ Chandos CHAN 8630)
♦ At a bargain price, Mravinsky's interpretation (⊗ on Leningrad Masters LM 1322) offers inimitable insights. Alas, the recording is dire even by Russian standards.

### Symphony No.11 in G minor, Opus 103: 'The Year 1905'
♦ Leningrad PO: Mravinsky (⊗ Praga PR254 018 – deletion imminent)

◆ Leningrad PO: Mravinsky (⊗ Russian Disc RD CD 11157 – 1957 recording)

### Symphony No.12 in D minor, Opus 112: 'The Year 1917'
◆ Leningrad PO, Mravinsky (⊗ Erato 2292-45754-2)
◆ Also commended (with *Symphony No.6*): Concertgebouw: Haitink (⊗ Decca 425 067-2DM)

### Symphony No.13 in B flat minor, Opus 113: 'Babi Yar'
◆ Kondrashin, Moscow PO, Eisen (bass), Choir of the Russian Republic (⊗ BMG Melodiya 74321198422)
◆ Digital recommendation: New York PO: Leiferkus (bass), Yevtushenko, New York Choral Artists, Masur (⊗ Teldec 4509-90848-2)

### Symphony No.14, Opus 135 for Soprano, Bass and Orchestra
◆ Vishnevskaya, Reshetin, MCO: Barshai (⊗ Russian Disc RD CD 11 192) with Oistrakh's old but lively performance of *Symphony No.9*
◆ Kasrashubili, Safiulin, USSR MoC SO: Rozhdestvensky (⊗ Olympia OCD 182) with Serov's recording of *King Lear*

### Symphony No.15 in A, Opus 141 (with orchestral version of the cycle 'From Jewish Folk Poetry', Opus 79)
◆ London PO: Haitink (⊗ Decca 425-069-2)

### Piano Concerto No.1 in C, Opus 35: Piano Concerto No.2 in F, Opus 102 (with Three Fantastic Dances, Opus 5: Preludes and Fugues, Opus 87 Nos.1, 4, 5, 23, 24)
◆ The composer (pf), Vaillant (tpt) / ONRF: Cluytens (⊗ EMI mono CDC 7 54606-2)
◆ Digital recommendation: (with '*The Assault on Beautiful Gorky*' from the Suite *The Unforgettable Year 1905*, Opus 89)
◆ Alexeev (pf), Jones (tpt) / ECO: Maksymiuk (⊗ EMI CD-CFP 4547)

## Violin Concerto No.1 in A minor, Opus 77 (issued as Opus 99)

♦ (with Prokofiev, *Violin Concerto No.1*) Vengerov (vln) / London SO: Rostropovich (⊗ Teldec 4509-92256-2)

## Violin Concerto No.2 in C sharp minor, Opus 129

♦ (with Shostakovich, *Violin Concerto No.1*) Mordkovitch (vln) / SNO: Järvi (⊗ Chandos CHAN 8820)

## Cello Concerto No.1 in E flat, Opus 107; Cello Concerto No.2, Opus 126

♦ Mork (vlc), London PO: Janssons
  (⊗ Virgin Classics VC 5 45145 2)
♦ Maisky (vlc), London SO: Thomas
  (⊗ DG 445 821-2)

## STAGE AND CINEMA WORKS

### The Bolt (complete – 2 CDs)

♦ RSPO, STB: Rozhdestvensky (⊗ Chandos CHAN 9343 / 4)

### The Golden Age (complete – 2 CDs)

♦ RSPO, Rozhdestvensky (⊗ Chandos CHAN 9251 / 2)

### Lady Macbeth of the Mtsensk District (complete – 2 CDs)

♦ Vishnevskaya, Gedda, Petrov; Ambrosian Opera Chorus, London PO / Rostropovich (⊗ EMI CDS 7 49955-2)

### Orchestral version of the cycle 'From Jewish Folk Poetry', Opus 79

♦ Söderström, Wenkel, Karczykowski, London PO: Haitink, (⊗ Decca 425-069-2 – with *Symphony No.15*)

### Mussorgsky, orchestrated by Shostakovich: Songs and Dances of Death

♦ Lloyd (bass): Philadelphia Orch: Janssons (⊗ EMI CDC 5 55232-2 – with Shostakovich, *Symphony No.10*)

## Suites for Film and Stage: The Gadfly, King Lear, Hamlet
♦    KRS SO: Jordana (⊗ Koch 3-7274-2H1)

## Five Ballet Suites, Suite from Katerina Ismailova, Festive Overture (2 CDs)
♦    SNO: Järvi (⊗ Chandos CHAN 7000 / 1)

### Abbreviations

| | |
|---|---|
| **BPO** | Berlin Philharmonic Orchestra |
| **DG** | Deutsche Grammophon |
| **MCO** | Moscow Chamber Orchestra |
| **MoC SO** | USSR Ministry of Culture Symphony Orchestra |
| oas | otherwise available separately |
| **ONRF** | Orchestre National de la Radiodiffusion Française |
| pf | piano |
| **PO** | Philharmonic Orchestra |
| **RSPO** | Royal Stockholm Philharmonic Orchestra |
| **SNO** | Scottish National Orchestra (also called RSNO) |
| **SO** | Symphony Orchestra |
| **STB** | Stockholm Transport Band |
| tpt | trumpet |
| vla | viola |
| vln | violin |
| vlc | cello |

# Index

# CLASSIC *f*M
# GARDEN PLANNER

## THE GARDENING FORUM TEAM:
## STEFAN BUCZACKI, FRED DOWNHAM, SUE PHILLIPS WITH DAPHNE LEDWARD

Drawing on 125 years of collective garden experience, the formidable *Cheltenham & Gloucester Classic Gardening Forum* team of Stefan Buczacki, Fred Downham and Sue Phillips with Daphne Ledward have created a stylish planner as a companion and adviser for all your garden needs.

The authors provide practical tips on subjects ranging from growing salad leaves in spring, cultivating late colour in borders and growing herbs, to creating spectacular hanging baskets and pots. There are checklists of things to do and regular features from team members discussing favourite plants, advice on special problems, and occasionally just a few words on the delights to be enjoyed in the garden.

Throughout, there is room for the reader to make notes or journal entries, or simply to reflect on a delightful day in the garden.

**£9.99**   ISBN: **1 85793 964 6**   **Paperback**

# CLASSIC *f*M

# MUSIC

## A JOY FOR LIFE

### EDWARD HEATH

### Foreword by Yehudi Menuhin

*Music* is a record of a lifetime's passion for a subject with which former Prime Minister Sir Edward Heath has been involved since he was nine years old. In this book – first published in 1976 and now updated in his eighty-first year – Sir Edward recalls his musical experiences, from his days as a chorister in his parish church to his work as a conductor of international renown – a career that began in 1971 when he conducted the London Symphony Orchestra playing Elgar's 'Cockaigne' Overture at its gala concert in the Royal Festival Hall.

From his friendships with Herbert von Karajan and Leonard Bernstein to his great musical loves such as Beethoven and British music, from music at Downing Street to a series of five symphony concerts he conducted for his eightieth birthday celebrations, Sir Edward gives a fascinating personal insight into his wide-ranging experience. Written with great knowledge and characteristic enthusiasm, *Music – A Joy for Life* will appeal both to those who already have a serious interest in music and also to those who enjoy music and would like a greater understanding.

£16.99   ISBN: 1 86205 090 2

# THE
# CLASSIC *f*M
# GUIDE TO
# CLASSICAL MUSIC

### JEREMY NICHOLAS
### Consultant Editor: ROBIN RAY
### Foreword by HUMPHREY BURTON

'... *a fascinating and accessible guide ... it will provide
an informative and illuminating source of insight
for everybody from the beginner to the musicologist.*'

Sir Edward Heath

*The Classic fM Guide to Classical Music* opens with a masterly
history of classical music, illustrated with charts and lifelines, and
is followed by a comprehensive guide to more than 500 composers. There are major entries detailing the lives and works of the
world's most celebrated composers, as well as concise biographies
of more than 300 others.

This invaluable companion to classical music combines extensive factual detail with fascinating anecdotes, and an insight
into the historical and musical influences of the great composers.
It also contains reviews and recommendations of the best works,
and extensive cross-references to lesser-known composers.
Jeremy Nicholas's vibrant, informative and carefully researched
text is complemented by photographs and cartoons, and is designed for easy reference, with a comprehensive index.

£19.99 ISBN: 1 85793 760 0 Hardback
£9.99 ISBN: 1 86205 051 1 Paperback

# CLASSIC *f*M
# LIFELINES

With 4.8 million listeners every week, *Classic fM* is now the most listened-to national commercial radio station in the UK. With the *Classic fM Lifelines*, Pavilion Books and *Classic fM* have created an affordable series of elegantly designed short biographies that will put everyone's favourite composers into focus.

Written with enthusiasm and in a highly accessible style, the *Classic fM Lifelines* series will become the Everyman of musical biographies. Titles for the series have been chosen from *Classic fM*'s own listener surveys of the most popular composers.

**£4.99 each book**

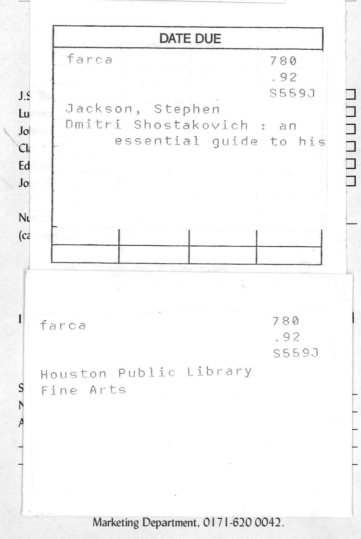

Marketing Department, 0171-620 0042.